Mrs. Carey Brock

Chapters on Bible Classes

Mrs. Carey Brock

Chapters on Bible Classes

ISBN/EAN: 9783337100339

Printed in Europe, USA, Canada, Australia, Japan

Cover: Foto ©Lupo / pixelio.de

More available books at **www.hansebooks.com**

CHAPTERS ON BIBLE CLASSES.

BY THE

AUTHOR OF "COPSLEY ANNALS,"

"THE END OF LIFE,"

"I MUST KEEP THE CHIMES GOING," ETC.

NEW YORK:
E. P. DUTTON & CO., 713, BROADWAY.
LONDON: SEELEY, JACKSON, & HALLIDAY.
1873.

PREFACE.

These "Chapters on Bible-Classes" originally appeared in the "Sunday School Teacher's Monthly Magazine." Their re-publication in a collective form has been carried out in accordance with many kindly requests.

In dedicating them to all Bible-class teachers who may be willing to accept such dedication, the writer cannot but express the conviction that there is on every side a call for more volunteers in this particular department of work. If in other divisions of labour a "missing link" has been discovered, there is surely, in too large a number of our parishes and districts, a link missing between the work of the Sunday School teacher and the minister,—a link which earnest and loving-hearted men and women are called to supply. We want more Bible-classes. We want *happy* Bible-classes. We want them in factory towns and in sea-side watering-places, and in "new districts," where the very un-home-like appearance of all things around makes the need for a home-like meeting such as a Bible-class ought to be, all the greater. We need them in scattered country neighbourhoods, how sorely those intimate with such neighbourhoods alone can tell; we need them beside railway stations, and among our shops; everywhere, indeed, there is a field for the exercise of that peculiar influence which, too often ceasing with the relationships of the Sunday School, may be so widely used for the extension around us of the Master's kingdom.

Should the following chapters be the means of animating to this field of labour some who may be content from small beginnings to work on hopefully, because of a living promise accompanying the sowing of a living Word, the aim with which they are sent forth will have been in no small measure attained.

September, 1872.

CONTENTS.

CHAPTER	PAGE
I. THE OBJECT AND STRUCTURE OF A BIBLE-CLASS.	1
II. PRE-REQUISITES OF THE BIBLE-CLASS TEACHER.	14
III. REQUISITES OF THE BIBLE-CLASS TEACHER.	25
IV. ON THE BEST METHOD OF CONDUCTING A BIBLE-CLASS	42
V. THE HOUR SET APART	59
VI. ON PREPARATION FOR ADULT BAPTISM	71
VII. ON PREPARATION FOR CONFIRMATION.	96
VIII. ON PREPARATION FOR THE LORD'S SUPPER	115
IX. ON BIBLE-CLASS FESTIVALS	147
X. BIBLE-CLASS CORRESPONDENCE .	158
XI. ON THE BEST METHOD OF EXCITING AND MAINTAINING A MISSIONARY SPIRIT IN THE BIBLE-CLASS	176

CHAPTERS ON BIBLE-CLASSES.

CHAPTER I.

THE OBJECT AND STRUCTURE OF A BIBLE-CLASS.

THE subject of Senior Bible-classes has been so frequently brought to the notice of earnest workers, that it might seem superfluous to make it the groundwork of a series of consecutive papers. But those who, from taking a keen personal interest in the matter, have dwelt thoughtfully on chapters already devoted to its consideration, will probably agree that we have had, after all, little more than a bird's-eye view of the subject. We have read of Bible-classes already formed; we have seen them in their working aspect; but the springs and wheels—the mechanism in its preparation and more continuous operation—have but scantily been laid before us; and we would inquire further. We would consider the formation and materials of the Bible-class, the qualifications and preparation of its teacher. We would not bid it farewell as it disperses on Sundays, but rather trace its influences as carried on through the week. The private intercourse between the teachers and the hearers, the preparations for Adult Baptism, Confirmation, Communion, all these are topics which must come before thorough-going workers; and to these subjects, and to others associated with them, we would give thoughtful and, it is hoped, suggestive attention.

If the notes here gathered, resulting from a deep sense of the blessings granted to a continuous setting forth of the living Word, with the expectation of power accompanying it from the influences of a present Spirit, may serve to remind some brothers or sisters struggling to carry on Bible-class work against the tide of adverse influences belonging to a town population, or in the yet more discouraging stagnation and isolation of many a country district, that they are not alone in their difficulties, anxieties, disappointments, and successes, but belong to a company with them bearing precious seed, and lifting up their eyes unto the hills from whence cometh help, they will at least fulfil a portion of the intention with which they are sent forth. It may be, also, that a notice of plans found useful in other Bible-classes will not be without value to those seeking suggestions for their work from these pages.

In the present chapter we propose considering the Objects and Formation of an Adult Bible-class.

And, firstly, *its object*.

In a certain sense we may undoubtedly say that one paramount object can alone be worthily aimed at in this, as in all other distinctive missionary work. It is clearly defined in Acts xxvi. 18: "To open their eyes, to turn them from darkness to light, and from the power of Satan unto God; that they may receive forgiveness of sins and inheritance among them which are sanctified by faith that is in Me."

We desire to convey *good impressions;* but there we can never be satisfied to remain. We are thankful if we obtain *seriousness of attention, observance of Sunday, church going;* but our aim is far beyond all these. CONVERSION, that actual transaction which cannot be carried out by proxy, that actual passage from death unto life, from the power of Satan unto God, compared with which every other transaction is immeasurably insignificant, and which takes place when there is an actual laying of sin upon the Sinbearer, an actual acceptance of pardon and imputed righteousness by the sinner,—this, and nothing less than this, must for each member of the class be the object, the prayer, the standard of the Christian teacher. It is a high standard; but can it be safely lowered? It is a high standard; but can every Bible-class teacher who reads these lines honestly say that he or she has so tried to its uttermost the power of faith, of prayer, and of constant exertion towards its attainment, as to be entitled to pronounce it an impossible one? We are quite sure that a high, *the highest*, aim in our teaching, accompanied though it continually must be by a deep sense of shortcoming, and a keen perception of every failure, is better, safer, and more really elevating than a lower standard more visibly attained. For instance, we think there is cause for uneasiness when the teacher of a Bible-class, after, it may be, some years of even attendance on that department of ministry, is satisfied with saying of its members, "They know their Bibles better; they answer better; they are more regular than they used to be." So far good! But what more? Is your object no higher? Is this all the result, all you expect from a living Word, from the promise of a living Spirit, from the intercession of a living Saviour, amongst those who must live for ever? Surely there must be some wide difference between such expectations and God's promises, between an improvement in outward observance and "life for our brethren." Surely by those thus easily satisfied, the "Prove me now, if I will not pour you out a blessing," of Him who is more ready to hear than we to pray, has not yet been presented for payment, not yet tested as a bond even now waiting to be claimed.

There are important subsidiary purposes which ought to be fulfilled by a well-organised Bible-class. For example, *as a means of leavening the district or parish to which it belongs*, its value cannot easily be over-estimated. Teaching received by actual or future parents must influence homes and children. Books circulated among its members spread the tide of influence. Visits, following up the general weekly instruction, bring together in cordial and affectionate intercourse the teachers and the hearers; and, as an established appendage to the Church and Church ministry, it may and should furnish from its ranks Sunday-school teachers, assistant visitors, and helpers in missionary and other organisations.

The last object upon which we may glance ere leaving this portion of our subject, is that which we desire to attain *in leading the members of a Bible-class to realise that, in belonging to it, they each make one of a community*, with common interests, pleasures, and responsibilities. There is, we are inclined to think, a feeling amongst most young persons, especially amongst those separated from their own homes, of desire to be "*in something*"—to belong to some body or company in which their natural impulses for companionship and interchange of acquaintance shall be associated with the dignities and freedom of grown-up life; and this should be supplied by a Bible-class such as that to which we aspire, especially if in it the elder members are willing to care for and interest themselves in the younger ones. The attainment of this object, on the basis of Christian fellowship, is in itself well worth trying for.

It remains to close this somewhat introductory chapter with a few words concerning *the structure* of a Bible-class.

It is almost unnecessary to observe, at the very outset, that locality, more than any other circumstance, must tend to decide this matter. The factory operatives of manufacturing towns, the farmers' daughters of rural districts, the "young women in business," and dressmakers and milliners of the West End, the scarcely reached ranks of male and female servants everywhere—all these, and hundreds of other classes of the community, are open to loving influences and kindly guidance.

But generalities are seldom helpful. Let us suppose a teacher, qualified, earnest, and sensible of the importance of the plan, desirous of establishing an adult class. How shall he enter on the scheme?

The first nucleus, common to most places, is that furnished by *boys and girls too old, or thinking themselves too old, for the Sunday-school.* The Sunday-school should have "*No Thoroughfare*" for its motto.

The little ones, admitted to the Infant gallery, and to the study of pictures of Daniel in the Lions' Den, and Joseph in the Pit, should be found, after many years, explaining New Testament allusions to Kings and Chronicles from their ranks in the senior classes, and ready at sixteen (for too low a standard of age lessens the dignity of the Bible-class) to be admitted formally and seriously as adult scholars. And if, ere conducting them to the Bible-class room, it is permitted to us to glance down the Sunday-school ranks through which they have passed during the interval, it would be to warn every teacher lest his or her class should prove to any child placed in it *a gap in the hedge* through which the little ones may be wont to stray into less wholesome pastures outside the fold carelessly guarded.

"And then you keep them in the Bible-class till they are married?" some inquirer will add.

Why "*till* they are married?" Why not *after* they are married? until, as is the case in a Bible-class now particularly in the thoughts of the writer, the feet of little ones pattering from the Sunday-school are heard outside the door, as they wait "till Bible-class is over for mother to come home"—that mother who herself ten or twelve years ago was in the upper class of their own dear Sunday-school.

But, not to digress, we have then, as a first nucleus,

the senior scholars of the Sunday-school. It is often a small one; in scanty populations a most uncertain one, since, especially in the country, the boys and girls are planted out in distant service almost as soon as they have left school. Where, then, shall we look for further materials?

At this point the nature of the population must, of course, be taken into consideration. It may be that in some densely-peopled factory district a room will be filled to its utmost limits by a single invitation published in the work-room with the consent of the mill-owners. It may be that in another parish an invitation from the clergyman will at once have the effect of inducing a large number of employers to encourage their servants to attend such a meeting. But this is not the general rule. "*Peu à peu*" is for the most part the teacher's motto in all things; and we are inclined to think that a gradually-formed and gradually-increasing Bible-class is likely to possess more of the elements of stability and success than one more suddenly and rapidly organised.

It need hardly be said that the countenance and co-operating influence of the clergyman of the district or parish should, if possible, be secured. This is as important on one side as it is, on the other, that the question of Church or Dissent should, as a test of admission, never for a moment be introduced. This co-operation will generally include permission to make use of his name as sanctioning requests to employers for the attendance of their servants, and will almost invariably invest the position of the class with a certain dignity furnishing an important accession of strength to the teacher.

Whether thus aided or not, our experience would go against what may be termed *class* invitations—those limiting the attendance to a certain section of society. Establish a "Servants' Bible Class," and dressmakers and milliners will, in all probability, hold themselves aloof, although housekeepers and upper servants, really in higher positions than the milliners' apprentices, might be among the attendants. Invite "milliners and dressmakers" especially, and they may, until reached by an influence which should entirely do away with such forms of class pride, look askance at the young under-servants. Have a class nominally for "young men in business," and a difficulty will arise in persuading the lads from the stable-yard over the way to look in, who might yet be led to a decision for life were they induced to join.

As a general rule, we would try and collect representatives of any section in the district whom we could persuade to come. A *Confirmation* in the parish will often furnish members. "We are going to talk about the Confirmation at the Bible-class; and as you think of being confirmed, I should be so glad if you would join us." A judicious district visitor may thus use the influence of a visit.

A week-day *Singing-class* is a feeder to the Bible-class, often telling most materially on its numbers. Let the former be bright and cheery. Let there be thoroughly pleasant part-songs—glees and choruses, if possible, with healthy, animating words; and then a shading off into sacred songs, into hymns, and chants which will help forward the church singing, together with some special hymn "for the Bible-class on Sunday." Those thus enlisted will probably wish to take their part when the Sunday arrives; and, were this paper intended as a record of personal experiences, instances could be furnished of those, thus first induced to join a Bible-class, who now, after years of attendance, look back upon their entrance among its ranks as their introduction to all that they most prize for time and for eternity.

"I came for the singing-class," said one whose passionate love for music was her sole inducement to join any of the district meetings, "and then I liked it all so much, that I thought I'd join the Bible-class too; but now that my husband and little children don't leave me time for both, I find I must give up one or the other."

"And which will you give up, Mrs. A. ?"

"The singing-class, ma'am. It's a great pleasure: but the Bible-class has taught me what I never knew before, and I couldn't miss that now, not for anything."

That was seven or eight years ago; and Mrs. A. is in the Bible-class still.

"I wish you'd come down to the Bible-class," was the conclusion of a "district visit" to Mrs. Johnson, up at the farm, who maintained a continual indifference to church, chapel, and every ordinance within reach. "We should be very glad to see you; and we've been having such nice singing lately, you'd like to hear it."

"Well, so they do say. They say you've got it up wonderful; and I've been thinking of coming down to hear you. I always was a one for a noise—always, before I was married; and I likes summut lively as much as ever."

Accordingly Mrs. Johnson appeared, and continued to appear; and it may be interesting to the reader to learn that her own part in the singing fully justified her verdict as to her personal taste.

A *Lending Library* in connection with the class—a library made up, not only of books which people *ought* to like, or "books suitable for the lower classes," but of books which they *do* like, and will read with pleasure, books with sparkle and narrative, as well as sound Christian teaching—is another tempting auxiliary.

Notices such as the following, sent home by the school children, or left, with a kind word, by members of the Bible-class undertaking the work, have been found very useful in inducing attendance,—at first, perhaps, from curiosity. It will be seen that they are invitations, in words slightly varied, to the same Bible-class: the first sent to the mothers of the school children, the second left from door to door by elder members of the class, themselves deeply in earnest in the work. It was found that an invitation, specially addressed to servants, was received by them more favourably than a general notice:—

(*General.*)

BIBLE READING FOR WOMEN.

You are cordially invited to the Bible Reading held every Sunday, from 2.30 to 3.30, in the Lower Room in Market Gardens.

The entrance is through the St. John's Church Enclosure, by the passage on the right.

When there is Evening Service at St. John's, the Bible Reading does not begin until 3 o'clock.

(*To Servants.*)

The Female Servants of St. John's District, and the adjoining neighbourhood, are cordially invited to the Bible Class held every Sunday, from 2.30 to 3.30, in the Lower Room in Market Gardens.

The entrance is through the St. John's Church Enclosure, by the passage on the right.

When there is Evening Service at St. John's, the Bible Class does not begin until 3 o'clock.

Succeeding papers may suggest other means of gaining attendance.

It will be sufficient, before closing, to meet with one word the objection: " Do not you find the mixture of ages and ranks attended with much difficulty ? Do not the members themselves dislike it ?"

To this there is but one reply. The teacher's personal influence should be sufficient to obviate any such difficulty. It should not be recognised as an impediment by any member of the class. Respect, genuine respect, shown to all, from the dullest and youngest, to the oldest, attendant, will arouse self-respect and will gain it from the rest; and a cheerful countenance, above all an earnest, loving spirit, reflecting that of the Master, will shine down and do away with class distinctions. At least it should do this, by God's help, —this, and very much more.

CHAPTER II.

PRE-REQUISITES OF THE BIBLE-CLASS TEACHER.

IN the course of a careful consideration of THE TEACHER'S REQUISITES, they have seemed so naturally to divide themselves into two parts, that the writer must be excused if, by thus placing them before the readers of these chapters, a lengthened trespass be made upon their time and attention. The question cannot but be regarded as one of deep practical importance; and it must be evident to all who have thoughtfully handled it, that the form of ministry represented by the charge and guidance of an adult Bible-class, demands, for its effective maintenance, *previously-possessed qualifications*—a stock-in-trade, so to speak, of *pre-*requisites, distinct from those working *requisites* acquired and called out in the exercise of the charge itself, and to be increasingly developed by such exercise. They are, however, few in number; and that which is of all others the most important stands, happily, within reach of the humblest aspirant for its possession.

What are, then, the *pre*-requisites for the effective Bible-class teacher?

"For spiritual work, spiritual agents!" This is a fundamental principle of one of our chief Missionary Societies; and it holds good in all grades of Missionary work, whether at home or abroad. We know of one only *indispensable* pre-requisite for the office of a Bible-class teacher. Many desirable qualifications may be considered in their places; but the one absolute necessity is that which can be furnished only from on high—that teaching of God's Holy Spirit which is *conversion*, the new birth of which the Lord of Life has said, "He that believeth on Me hath everlasting life." And, therefore, it needs that every teacher, and very specially each one proposing himself or herself for this work of Adult Classes, should make solemn and earnest heart-inquiry as to the reality of this work of God in the soul.

There may be a sense of the solemnity of eternal things; but this is not conversion.

There may be unfeigned desire for the good of others; but this does not necessarily imply change of heart.

There may be willingness to undergo fatigue and inconvenience in what is called "doing good," and yet no life in the soul; nothing but kind and generous impulse — a phosphorescence of energy, instead of God's light shining on the face of the waters.

This is, perhaps, hardly the place for entering at full length upon the subject which lies at the root of all that we can possibly write or say concerning Bible-class teaching. It may be best touched by leaving the following questions, in all their weighty import, for the consideration of those who may read these words; and on the pages of their own Bibles they will find unfailing counsel in their consideration:—

1. Have I seen myself to be lost,—under sentence of death,—born under a curse,—guilty before God,—and of myself unable to save myself?

2. Have I seen that in my stead Christ, on the cross, suffered the extremity of the penalty due to my sins —that He, Himself, bore my sins in His own body on the tree, thus, having borne the curse for me, setting me entirely free from its load?

3. Has that transaction passed between me and an unseen living Saviour which decides my eternity? Have I taken hold of His death as my own title to life? Have I accepted His sacrifice as *for me*, hearing Him say, "Him that cometh unto me I will in no wise cast out," and replying with my whole heart, "O Lamb of God, I come?"

4. Have I given myself wholly and entirely to Him who gave Himself for me; taking Him as my Lord, my Guide, my Example, my All; looking for His hand to lead, and listening for His voice to direct me, and enjoying that fellowship which is with the Father and His Son Jesus Christ, and into which we are admitted, through the blood of Jesus Christ which cleanseth us from all sin? And have I His service and glory as my one object?

These questions are solemn ones, and they are of all importance. They represent the transition from death unto life—that real, actual passage from the kingdom of Satan into the kingdom of God's dear Son, which is entrance into His glorious light. Can they, then, be passed over? Oh that every teacher reading these pages might know the full blessedness of conscious acceptance and sonship!

We say of *conscious* acceptance; for how can a person throw out a rope to others sinking in the flood unless his own standing be firm and secure? We believe that half the reason of non-success amongst really converted teachers arises from their not realising the "strength of their salvation;" their absolute security in Christ; the high position in which those are placed who stand "accepted in the Beloved." If assurance is "presumption," then taking God at His word is presumption, and regarding the Lord's own words, "is passed from death unto life" as a mistake on His part who has the keys of life and death, is the attitude of faith.

Oh, why are people willing to lose their birthright of assurance when they have the title-deeds in their own possession? You have been translated into a new region, dear brother or sister, who have laid your sins on Jesus, and who have given your lives to Him. It is called the Land of pardon and peace. It is a fair country; and yet you are willing to stand only just within its frontier, content to leave unexplored one point of view after another whence you might see in fresh lights the extent of your liberties and your privileges—whence you might gain brightest glimpses of the Celestial City. "Walk about Zion, and go round about her, and tell the towers thereof; mark ye well her bulwarks, consider her palaces, *that ye may tell it to the generation following;*" and then, from the full consciousness of *having come* unto Mount Zion, of having joined yourself to the city of the living God, you will be able to exclaim, without a shadow of mistrust, and from the security of her pavilions, "This God is our God *for ever and ever; He will be our guide unto death.*"

"I have never, to my knowledge, brought a single soul to Christ," is the mournful complaint of one really trusting in His merits, and saved through His death.

"But, dear friend, have you ever been able to say to

others, '*I* am happy; *I* have found peace; the fear of death has been taken away from *me; I* know Christ as a present Saviour?"

"No, I cannot say all this; but I can truly say that I have no trust but in Him."

And is it not often thus, that "no trust except in Christ" falls very far short of full and realised trust in Christ? And yet full and conscious dependence on His word of welcome can alone enable us to bring others to "like precious faith with us *through the righteousness of God and our Saviour Jesus Christ.*"

"Is it not wonderful that all this should be for you and me?" said—one Sunday afternoon as they walked home together—the teacher of a Bible class to one of the members, herself brought through its means some years before to the knowledge of Jesus. The subject had been the safety and glorious inheritance of the believer.

"And yet if we did not believe it we should make God a liar," was the answer.

And so it is, Christian teacher; you cannot be a happy teacher, and you can never be a really successful one, unless you are able to say, boldly and fearlessly, "*I* believed not the words until I came, and mine eyes had seen it; and behold, the half was not told me."

"I waited patiently for the Lord, and He inclined unto me, and heard my cry. He brought me up also out of an horrible pit, and *set my feet upon a rock, and established my goings.* And He hath put a new song in my mouth, even praise unto our God."

And then "many shall see it and fear, and shall put their trust in the Lord;" teachers and hearers together joining in the chorus meetly following such a strain of rejoicing: "Blessed is that man that maketh the Lord his trust."

A power of sympathy is both a requisite and pre-requisite for the successful teacher. We do not only mean sympathy as shown in times of sickness or sorrow befalling individual members of a Bible-class, but the rarer qualification of *sympathy in teaching.* The leader of the class should feel himself, while teaching, to be two distinct persons—the teacher and the taught. He should be able to see unspoken difficulty in the countenances of his hearers; nay, more, should *feel* a difficulty for them before it has had time to betray itself in their faces, so that they shall find it anticipated and smoothed away, it may be, ere taking a distinct form. *Fidgety* inattention hardly ever presents itself as a Bible-class difficulty. It has been left behind as the lively foe of the Sunday-school teacher. A sort of earthwork of quiet, orderly stolidity, harder to meet than active impatience, is the intrenchment to penetrate which the Bible-class teacher must exert his efforts. A single glance directed to where a hearer is flapping the pages of his hymn-book, or playing with her gloves, will, in an Adult Class, be sufficient, in all probability, to put a stop to the inattentive gesture; but tact, and sympathy, and energy, and inflections of voice, and changes of manner,—all these, and twenty other nameless resources, on the part of the teacher, must be called out if the teaching is to tell, and to carry further than " the song of one that hath a pleasant voice, and can play well on an instrument."

It is almost impossible to *describe* a power which must be *felt* rather than seen. St. Paul eminently possessed it. How he identified himself with the difficulties of his hearers! pausing, at each new position in his arguments, to look back, and to carry up the intelligences of his auditors to his own standing-point, with a question, or with a summary of the steps already gained:—

"What advantage, then, hath the Jew?" "What shall we say, then, that Abraham our father hath found?" "What shall we say, then? shall we continue in sin that grace may abound? God forbid!" "Know ye not, brethren (for I speak to them that know the law)." "I say, then, hath God cast away His people?" "Thou wilt say, then, the branches were broken off that I might be grafted in! Well, because of unbelief they *were* broken off." "But some man will say, How are the dead raised up?" &c.

This style of teaching, accompanied, as it evidently was, by a powerful manner,—the stretching forth of the hand, the impulsive, winning, "King Agrippa, believest thou the prophets? *I know that thou believest!*"—betrays a power of sympathy in teaching of the very highest order, a power which every teacher should earnestly seek to acquire. That it can be acquired, in less or greater degree, we have little doubt. Close and earnest observation of the needs and difficulties of one's hearers, combined with a very loving spirit, and with a strong desire to help, is a good beginning; and no better school than Sunday-school teaching can be suggested for its culture. That there should be *something* of it in possession,—enough to become very much more,—we are inclined to consider almost a necessary to success as a Bible-class teacher.

Superiority in social position, or, at least, *in education*, if not an indispensable, is undoubtedly a most important advantage to the teacher. In many of our northern Sunday-schools there is a spirit of radicalism which can be met only by these qualifications in combination, until there has been time for the growth of that personal affection—we would hope, also for that reverence for a holy life and purpose—which will, more surely than any other tie, bind together the teachers and the taught. Members of the clergyman's or the squire's family, sons or daughters of the mill-owners whose "hands" have souls to be loved and cared for, teachers from among the resident gentry, cannot over-estimate the value of a position which it may be theirs to constitute one of influence for Christ.

Examples from higher stations, of talents, of position and influence, thus cast into the treasury, are happily not wanting in our own day.

"I often wish," was lately the observation of a young woman in whose heart the seed sown, though it had for some time appeared to lie dormant, had been quickened into life,—"I often wish now that his lordship" (referring to the Earl of C.) "could know all the good his teaching has been to me. He was my Sunday-school teacher at home, and took ever so much pains with me; but I didn't profit as I should at the time. And now all he taught me seems to come back and help me on every day."

"I do not come among you as the Right Hon. Lord Haddo," said the late Earl of Aberdeen—referring, in an address, to a bill announcing his promise to preside at a Sunday-school Teachers' Meeting, "but as one who has been a Sunday-school teacher; and I must request that, if at any future meeting I can be of use to you by presiding, the advertising notice of it shall be expressed thus :—" The Chair will be taken by a Sunday-school Teacher.'"

In the long run, however, education and ability, as

qualifications for the superintendent of an Adult Class, will, if combined with Christian lovingness and purpose, have as much weight as superiority of social position; probably more. Unconsciously, teaching stamped with the authority of truth and of superior information will command growing respect and attention. Indeed, concerning every gift and accomplishment, all power of illustration, and form and variety of thought, it may be generally said that, as around the wire introduced into the clouded chemical solution there form instantly crystals, perfect in form and delicate in beauty, so *definite purpose for Christ* will attract, and group around it for the Master's work, all that which might otherwise lie, useful but unutilised, in heart and mind. Only let us take as our motto and watchword concerning every social, mental, and intellectual possession, the dignified and all-constraining "UNTO THE LORD," and many a power which before we had hardly recognised, and of which, it may be, none around us had taken knowledge, will present itself to our consciousness crystallised for service.

CHAPTER III.

REQUISITES OF THE BIBLE-CLASS TEACHER.

THE *pre*-requisites of the Bible-class teacher formed the subject of our last chapter. We now proceed to consider what we may call the *working requisites* for the conduct of such a charge—requirements as needful for carrying it on successfully, as the fire and the steam to the engineer who would guide the train faithfully in the course laid down for it.

Need we say that far before any other requisite stands that of *expectant prayer?*

"Will you join a prayer-meeting intended for those who expect to get what they pray for?" Such was the invitation received a short time ago from a friend, himself eminent amongst expectant and receiving petitioners. If we were to judge from the tenour of the New Testament, with the "Ask, and ye shall receive" of a living Saviour echoed throughout its pages, would it not seem that every Christian must, as a matter of course, be included in such an invitation? If we judge from realities—above all, from the weakness of our own faith—do we not read a contrary testimony?

Expectant prayers are, we fear, comparatively exceptional amongst us who hold the bond on an inexhaustible exchequer, "What things soever ye ask in faith, believing, ye shall receive;" and yet, assuredly, *answered prayers* are the Christian's jewels—gems of surpassing value laid by for continual reviewal and estimation.

A few lines on this subject from the pen of Archbishop Leighton have always struck us as so full of beauty and encouragement that we cannot refrain from introducing them to the notice of our readers:—" He that is much in prayer shall grow rich in grace. He shall thrive and increase most, who is busiest in this, which is our very traffic with heaven, and fetches our most precious commodities thence. He who sends oftenest out these 'ships of desire,' who makes the most voyages to that land of spices and pearls, shall be sure to improve his stock most, and have most of heaven upon earth."

Shall we not be inclined to exclaim, with the pious writer in the next sentence, "But the true art of this trading is very rare?"

To bring this subject, however, to bear especially on

REQUISITES OF THE BIBLE-CLASS TEACHER. 27

the point under consideration, we would urge the bringing to the ear of Him who seeth in secret every confidence, every detail, every disappointment, every dawning of hope concerning our Bible-class work. The thought of being "labourers together with God" is a marvellous support in such work. "*Obtained promises*" holds high rank amongst the great achievements of faith chronicled in the 11th of the Hebrews, standing in order with the records of those who subdued kingdoms and wrought righteousness.

For us, in our relationship to our Bible-classes, there is a solemn warning in Samuel's words: "God forbid that I should sin in ceasing to pray for you!" And the following anecdote, taken from a book which has had some circulation amongst Sunday-school teachers, may be here cited, as containing striking encouragement to earnest and expectant prayers:—

"A pious young lady was requested to teach a class of girls in a Sabbath-school in New York. She accepted the invitation, and engaged in the work. She was seen to be very earnest, faithful, and affectionate with her youthful charge. In a little while one scholar after another became thoughtful, serious, and anxious, until every member of her class was converted to God. She was then requested to give up her class and take another in which none of the scholars were earnest. After due consideration, she consented. She had not been long in her new class before similar effects were produced, and ultimately every member of the class cherished hope in Christ. She was finally induced to give up this class also, and take another class of children *who were unconverted*. She had not laboured long when precisely the same results as before followed her labours. Every scholar in the class became in earnest. Her work was now done. She fell asleep in Jesus, and entered the rest that remaineth for the people of God.

"After her death, her friends, on examining her journal, found the following resolution :—'Resolved, that *I will pray once each day for my class by name!*'

"On looking further into the journal, they found the same resolution, re-written and re-adopted, with a slight addition, as follows : —'Resolved, that I will pray over each member of my class by name, and *agonise in prayer!*'

"On looking still further into the journal, the same resolution was found, with a fresh addition :—'Resolved, that I will pray once each day for each member of my class by name, and agonise in prayer; *and that I will expect a blessing!*'"

Very distinct are promises made to believing intercession. If we, who are Bible-class teachers, are failing to obtain "life for our brethren," is there no omission lying at our door? Let us seek to be able in our turn to write beneath such promises, "Tried and proved."

Earnest study of the Scriptures is another requisite upon which chapters, rather than pages, might be written.

Some years ago, a clergyman, acting as Deputation for the Irish Church Missions, preached to an educated congregation in a fashionable town. In the course of his sermon, he was led to describe a visit to an Irish Ragged-school under Protestant instruction; and, as a proof of the care with which the scholars had been taught, he said, "I asked them what became of the bodies of the men slain in Ishmael's conspiracy? and the answer was given in a moment. Now," continued the preacher, "I leave it to each member of this congregation, whether he or she could at this instant furnish the reply to that question."

In the Sunday-school, that afternoon, there was a whispering among the teachers collected before the opening. "Do *you* know?" "Can *you* tell?" "Have *you* found out?"—was passing from one to another. Suddenly the door of the girls'-school opened, and the curate—a valued friend of all the teachers—went up, his open Bible in his hand, to the superintendent's desk: "Miss ——, you are sure to know: do tell me where it is!" Alas! Miss —— could not remember: and clergyman and teachers acknowledged to each other that they had themselves received a lesson not to be forgotten. We hand on the test to the readers of these pages.

We fear that there is, among teachers, a great lack of knowledge of Scripture *as a whole;* and here we are speaking of critical and head knowledge, to be gained by force of research and earnest study, rather than of that supernatural teaching which comes from the Holy Spirit's influence, in whose light we can alone see light.

At a church not very far removed from the one already mentioned, the incumbent, while speaking one day on this subject, remarked, "I wonder which of this congregation could at once give a correct list of all the Minor Prophets!" Many of his hearers acknowledged to going home heartily ashamed of themselves. If the Bible is held by us as a revelation from God Himself, does it not seem incredible that it should be so little studied? At a rough calculation, many young ladies give more than one-eighth of their time to the practice of music, independently of any other acquirements. And what is the proportion of time and study devoted to other amusements and accomplishments, in comparison with what is given, and what is absolutely necessary, for anything more than a superficial knowledge of the Word of God?

How many of us teachers could draw from memory a plan of the Tabernacle, with its furniture, illustrating its types from the New Testament? How many could tell the points at which profane history first touches sacred history, and those at which it crosses and recrosses the thread of Scripture narrative? Could we readily answer an inquiry as to the respective works of Zerubbabel, Ezra, and Nehemiah, and the occasions on which the ministry of the latter combined? Could we write from memory a connected history of any one of the five last Jewish kings? or specify the dates and occasions of the various deportations into captivity, or of the different distinct missions of the prophets? Could we connectedly account for the close of the Old Testament in the reign of the Persian kings, and the opening of the New Testament, with Herod of Edom for a king, and Rome for a sovereign power? Could we analyse, as a subject long thought out, the plan of the Sermon on the Mount? or give the origin of the Feast of the Dedication, when Jesus walked in Solomon's Porch? or write out in order the history and travels of St. Paul? or trace out connectedly through his Epistles the evidences and testimony to his having received direct teaching from the Lord Himself?

These tests are not proposed with an idea of discouraging teachers who have not had time or books for so close a study of Scripture as others more favourably circumstanced, but rather as opening out subjects behind which lie important fields of knowledge, yielding rich harvests to the student. *Thoroughness* is so important a qualification for all, but most especially for those desiring the office of a teacher, that it is not too much to say that a great deal of the disinclination to the reading of the Bible, which is common amongst us, is the result of our having so scantily mastered what we may call the *secular* study of Scripture. The Artesian wells must be sunk, often with labour and difficulty, before a whole stream of refreshing water rushes from beneath the apparently dry soil for the reward of the undaunted worker.

We would advise those who have time, and who can by any means obtain the help of proper books, to spare no pains in acquiring such a knowledge of contemporary profane history as shall be, if we may so call it, a thorough backbone to their Scripture history; to seek to gain such a knowledge of the Bible historical books as shall cause the writings of the prophets to start into life-like pictures before them of the reigns of kings, whose lives, sometimes very perplexed, they have disentangled and smoothed out after careful study of the Kings and Chronicles. The attempt to harmonise our Lord's history, as given by the four Evangelists, even though it be impossible to execute it with perfect accuracy, will be attended with a great deal of good; and important assistance may be obtained from well-chosen books in every department of these studies.

It may be useful to the reader to be told of some books specially helpful to teachers.

Pre-eminent as a help to critical study of the Scriptures, stand Smith's *Old and New Testament Histories*, in two volumes. Of course many less expensive books might be obtained, but none probably really comparable in the research and variety of its contents, of a size to be within reach of most teachers. Eadie's *Bible Dictionary*, Horne's *Introduction to the Study of the Scriptures*, Calmet's *Biblical Dictionary*, Kitto's *Bible Encyclo-*

pædia, and many others, are most valuable in their way; but the modern researches of Rawlinson and others are in the first-mentioned volumes presented ready for use, in a manner to be quickly grasped by the reader.

The Religious Tract Society's compiled *Commentary* is excellent; Matthew Henry's *Commentary* gives us, perhaps, more than others of "the expressed juice of the grape"—the actual essence of the Scripture thought. It need hardly be added, that Conybeare and Howson's *Life and Epistles of St. Paul* is a book beyond all price for the student of the Acts and Epistles; while the *Notes of Lessons* published by the Church of England Sunday School Institute offer to the teacher advantages and assistance of no common kind.

But more important than this critical knowledge of our Holy Bible is that supernatural teaching of the Spirit of God, even now granted to those who seek it. One may, in the highest respect, be a successful teacher without the more elaborate scholarly study of the Bible; but without this last it is impossible permanently to touch the hearts of others. As for the development of the invisible ink, in which we now so commonly write our secret postal messages, light and heat are needed,—so, for the revealing of the thoughts of Christ in His Word to the heart of the reader, the light and warmth of the Holy Spirit are absolutely necessary. Otherwise it must be a blank letter, an unread message, to us all our lives.

And may not many of us who are teachers testify to the glories of the spiritual landscape when that Holy Spirit comes with life and light to "chase the dark clouds of mist away?"—when the grandeur of Christ's atonement, and the high dignities of the "accepted in the Beloved," and the far glimmerings of the glory in the distance, come into sight, revealed by His own illumination of the Word? Our testimony, when, having thus been taught ourselves, we prepare to declare unto others that which we have heard, which we have seen with our eyes, which we have looked upon of the Word of Life, will be that of Dr. Chalmers, in an anecdote, characteristic in force and interest, belonging to the period when he, after long conflict, had passed from death unto life :—

"His nearest neighbour and frequent visitor at Kilmany was old John Bonthron, who, having once seen better days, was admitted to an easy and privileged familiarity. In the exercise of this, one day, before the memorable illness which was the turning-point in the history of his minister, he said to Mr. Chalmers, 'I find you aye busy, sir, with one thing or another; but, come when I may, I never find you at your studies for the Sabbath.' 'Oh, an hour or two on Saturday evening is quite enough for that,' was the minister's answer. But now the change had come, and John, on entering the manse, often found Mr. Chalmers poring eagerly over the pages of the Bible. The difference was too striking to escape notice; and with the freedom given him he said, 'I never come now, sir, but I find you aye at your Bible.' 'All too little, John; all too little!' was the significant reply."

A more than common amount of *Perseverance* is a requisite for the Bible-class teacher. Of course this applies peculiarly to all teachers, and indeed to all who have any kind of work in the world. But in our department we know that, as far as human instruction goes, the teaching given in the Bible-class is probably final;—that as in the factory the vessel which has received, in one department and another, form, and colour, and patient moulding, remains in the hands and under the supervision of the final artificers until pronounced ready for service,—so we must unweariedly seek so to care for, and follow out, the individual case of each one of our charge, as that nothing shall be wanting on our part for the preparation of a vessel "meet for the Master's use."

It *does* require much determined perseverance to seek to know and teach individually and privately those less intelligent, or, it may be, unimpressible members of a class who seem to offer little hope of being influenced for good. But no class will prosper unless thus built up—unless each of its attendants is able to feel, "My teacher thinks of me, and cares for me, and looks after me, and writes to me, just as if there wasn't any one but me in the class to think of." Oh, how many instances could the writer give, from one Bible-class and another, of the rich return granted to unflagging perseverance in following up the teaching among the "*dull*" members of the little band! and how earnest should we be, how persevering in prayer, that none may go forth from us without having the stamp of the Master's acceptance and adoption!

Another requisite upon which we would touch is that of *method* in the work. We would pass it over as so completely a matter of course as hardly to need mention, were it not that it is a qualification which should be gradually displayed in Bible-class work. We require a sort of *veiled method* for carrying out our plans, and for this reason :—

The Bible-class is made up in part of scholars passed on to us from the Sunday-school, who are accustomed to the clockwork regularity, the carefully marked register, the firm, methodical rule of Superintendent and Teachers, and who associate such outward signs of routine with being "sent to school." But Bible-class attendance generally is, and ought to be, entirely voluntary, and should be felt as such. Outward similarity to school routine should be as much avoided as possible. The respect due to grown-up friends should be consciously felt as received from the teacher the moment the Sunday-scholar crosses the threshold of the Bible-class room; and its members should realise that to them has come the responsibility of maintaining, by regularity, serious attention, and general deportment, the dignity of the Adult-class. Give a *public* reproof in a Bible-class for late attendance, and you run the risk of losing the scholar; make a marked display of attendance registers, of remembering irregularities of attendance, &c., and grown-up members of families, married men and women, persons in independent positions, will not come.

But we would not be misunderstood. Underneath all, and consciously to ourselves, let there be exact, although *elastic*, method. Let lessons be given on the most methodical plans; only let them at all times be capable of expansion and special adaptation. Let registers be in private methodically kept. Let punctuality on the teacher's part be unvarying. Let visits be methodically paid, and correspondence methodically carried on; only let such method be *felt* and not *seen*, the framework realised, but not observed, which lies under all that is loving and indulgent and sympathising on the part of the teacher. The carrying out of this subject belongs, however, more properly to our next chapter.

We shall use the expression *enthusiasm* in the course of these chapters, and we would venture to dwell for a moment on our intention in so doing. Are we wrong in our belief that there is among us, as teachers, a want of enthusiasm in our actual teaching? There is love—love to Christ and love to souls. There is pleading for the Holy Spirit, that the fire from above may descend upon the work. There is earnestness. There is self-denial. All these—the *essential* requisites—have been through God's goodness given to many who will read these pages. But, in addition to these higher qualifications, we shall find that the mixture of spirit, of admiration, of natural interest, of sparkle, of ardour, of energy, and of everything else which goes to the compounding of that which we call enthusiasm, will tell a long way in exciting the sympathy and interest which we so desire to secure. We must not be content to dwell on the dignified heights of teachership, but must come down and learn with our classes, must admire with them, wonder with them, and enjoy with them. The secret of the success achieved by a famous captain, in contrast with the non-success of others, was said to lie in that, while their word of action was "*Go on!*" his was "*Come on!*" and we shall do well to remember that an honest, natural expression of fellow-feeling —"Don't you enjoy this passage?" "Isn't that expression beautiful?" "I hope we shall have time for that verse, for I am longing to come to it!" kindles our hearers into quick fellow-feeling.

Such vivid interest spreads rapidly from teacher to learners. In a Bible-class of about eighteen young women, held many years ago on Sunday mornings, the course of instructions was upon the Tabernacle. The teacher, intensely interested in the subject, spared no pains in bringing before them the wonderful types belonging to it, in pourtraying and illustrating every point of its construction, and in making the slowest of the class enter, New Testament in hand, into its teachings. Her eagerness spread to its members, and they studied the subject at home. On a certain Sunday morning the door of the class-room opened, and one of the members entered, followed by some others, bearing with much care a beautifully-constructed cardboard model of the Tabernacle, with its court, outer court, altars, laver, &c., made entirely by herself, and with no guide but her Bible and her teacher's instructions; and this she gratefully presented as an acknowledgment of her own and her companions' appreciation of the Tabernacle lessons. The same subject was being explained in the Boys' Bible-class, and news of the model spread to its members. One of them, the son of a carpenter, not to be outdone, and keenly interested in his own teacher's explanation, set to work on a yet more elaborate construction, and proudly presented her with a wooden model, perfectly proportioned, as the esult of his labours.

Nothing of the real dignity of the teacher will be lost by this fervour in teaching, which binds into a union of feeling both teacher and hearers. Neither will an occasional gleam of humour, kindling a smile throughout the whole class, if at a proper time and under the teacher's complete control, detract from the reverence due to the day and the occasion. On the contrary, a quick ripple of smiling appreciation, following some illustrative anecdote, often breaks the dead calm of respectful stolidity; and a sudden touch of humour flashing into the class will not unfrequently furrow up the line of dull earth which seemed to resist tillage, leaving it ready for softer and gentler influences. For we are so constituted, so sensitively moulded— heart vibrating to heart, and string to string—that the realisation of our human kinship must underlie and enter into every part of our teaching, if it is to be lasting and binding.

It only remains to add, that the all-important requisites of deep heart-felt *love* and *lovingness* (for there is a distinction) are so obvious and so pre-eminent, that they are only touched upon in conclusion as summing up all remaining qualifications for the Bible-class teacher, as well as having been implied in every one of those pre-requisites considered in our last chapter. Close converse and intimate union with our present Lord must result in such a loving reflection of His image as shall draw our hearers to His side.

"What has made you want to be a real Christian?" was the question once asked of a Bible-class attendant who called late one night at her teacher's house, the one burden of her visit being, "I want to be a real Christian, and I don't seem to know how!"

"It's seeing how happy they all look in the Bible-class who can say they've found Jesus," was the answer.

And should not this be the testimony concerning all of us who would win souls for our Master? Should not our love, sympathy, earnestness, joy and peace in believing, gain for us from those whom we teach the same testimony? should not they thus "take knowledge of us, that we have been with Jesus?"

CHAPTER IV.

ON THE BEST METHOD OF CONDUCTING A BIBLE-CLASS.

THE best *time* for holding the class will, of course, be decided by local circumstances, and, if assembled on Sunday, by the hours at which Church service is held. When the larger number of Bible-class members attend Afternoon service, the best time will probably be that immediately preceding its commencement, so that there shall be a general move to it from the Bible-class room. More fortunately are those circumstanced who, from the opportunity of attending Evening service, have the undisturbed afternoon before them, and who thus avoid a certain measure of hurry, and a crowding of ordinances which almost always attends the holding of a Bible-class immediately before church. As regards the length of time which may be wisely apportioned to its exercises, we would incline to the opinion that it should not be less than an hour, nor more than an hour and a quarter.

As regards the *place* of meeting, there will generally be circumstances determining the matter in each individual case. We would only advise that the Bible-class room should, if possible, be entirely separate from the school, unless the class be held at a time when there is no school going on, and when, consequently, the school-rooms are available for use. If held in a private room at the Rectory, or at some country house, we would advise that the place of meeting should be as near as possible to the outer door, and as much as possible a *parish* room. Easy access, a boarded floor, comfortable forms, and the various accessories of a place of common interest, will induce many to attend who would shrink from "looking in for a Sunday," by way of experiment, were there the many passages, the mahogany chairs, the pier-glasses, and carpeted floor, and a measure of "best room" state in their ideas attaching to the furniture of an ordinary dining-room. It may be, however, in some parishes a necessity that the Bible-class should be held in a class-room, and at the same hour as the Sunday-school. Should such be the case, every pains should be taken by the teacher to let its members feel that they have passed as real a boundary as if half a mile intervened between the buildings—that they have stepped into a community of which the dignity is thoroughly respected, a community bound by voluntary attendance only, held together by mutual love and desire after one high object, and upon which devolves the responsibility of individually and collectively supporting the teacher in his work, and maintaining the tone and influence of the class.

In some schools there is a habit of uniting the Adult class with the ordinary school-classes for the opening hymn and prayer. If the Bible-class consists only of ex-scholars there may not be indiscretion in such a plan; but we doubt whether outsiders—young men and young women sensitive to a laugh at their "going to school again," or fathers and mothers of the children—would ever be induced to join adult classes thus opened; and the teachers of such classes must acquire, if they are not already fortunate enough to possess it, an intuitive perception for a whole assortment of "feelings," some of them very foolish, and, consequently, very strongly rooted, which will only melt away before a sunshiny lovingness, and a keenly reciprocated personal respect shown to, and felt by, every member of the class.

It need hardly be added that the entrance to the Bible-class room should never be through the Sunday-school. Ease of access from without is a requisite which sounds trifling to the inexperienced teacher only. Those who have been long in the work know what an inducement to that all-important step, *a first attendance,* is a door opening into the street, and will give every opportunity for an undecided listener, perhaps afterwards to become an earnest and regular attendant, to "slip in unbeknownst." "I made up my mind to come," was the confession, after years had passed by, of such a hearer, who half stealthily crept into a Bible-class, open to all, induced to go and see what it was like from having taken an interest in the teacher, frequently encountered out of doors: "I wouldn't have gone if they hadn't said I could slip out if I didn't like it, and no one would take any notice." It pleased God that this first attendance should be the first step towards the knowledge of a Saviour, who, through the teaching of that Bible-class, revealed Himself to the furtive inquirer. That hearer, now a devoted and most successful missionary labourer, through the week engaged in bringing the gospel to poverty-stricken courts and close alleys, and still Sunday by Sunday to be found in the class at first thus furtively joined, is now one of its oldest members, and to its teacher and members brings an influence and example which have proved to them a constant help and blessing.

We have now arrived at the actual point of conducting the proceedings during the hour of attendance. And before entering upon this part of our subject, we may, perhaps, be permitted to refer to the remarks in the chapter immediately preceding concerning the method and system desirable for a Bible-class. We there observed that any conspicuous display of rules, or imposing production of registers and systematic machinery, ought to be avoided in the management of an adult class. But, on the other hand, we would say to every teacher, let your books be privately kept in the most orderly and systematic manner possible,— your roll of names, and a yet more private book with personal notices of visits to and from members, together with a supplementary list of those leaving the class, with their addresses. In a large class, numbering, say, from thirty upwards, it would be nearly impossible to be certain of accurately noting individual attendance without a regular calling over; but a teacher with a quick eye and memory will generally be able to write down memoranda immediately afterwards sufficient as a guide for visits to non-attendants, inquiries as to sick members, &c.

It is a good plan to make one member responsible in such a Bible-class for quietly, and without attracting notice, counting, Sunday by Sunday, the numbers present, and reporting them to the teacher; but a regular calling over will give a certain Sunday-school air to the proceedings; will make those who have been unable to come in time feel shy at appearing, or choose the alternative of staying away altogether, if prevented by business from arriving before the opening prayer; and will often, by its publication of names, cause some sensitive or undecided ones to renounce every idea of attendance "if their names are to be read out loud before all the rest."

In one Bible-class, numbering more than a hundred members, and which has been established for many years, the names are twice a year read over by the teacher somewhat in this fashion:—" Before we part, I must ask if you will kindly help me to correct any mistake which may have crept into the class list, which, as you know, I am anxious to keep correctly. It would be a great disappointment to me if, through any fault of mine, I should omit to send an invitation to our tea party to any member; and as I was away for two or three weeks in the spring (or autumn), it is quite possible that some may have gone or some come without my having entered the names. I need hardly say that the names are always entered in the order in which members join the class." The names are then rapidly read, fellow-servants or friends present helping the teacher to make any corrections, and a perfectly faultless list is ready for fresh copying. Copies of the roll of names are also kept by two or three of the longest established and leading members of the class, who visit amongst the rest, and who amongst themselves and each other conduct a little association for working for the very poor. This proof of the teacher's assurance of their sympathy and co-operation is much valued; and the possession of a class-list enables them to help out many a plan for the good of all, and to assist very materially in the work of looking up absentees.

The question will at this point arise, "Is it not very possible that there may thus be in actual attendance at a large Bible-class some who have never been regularly admitted by the teacher? And would not such irregular attendance be against one's ideas of order and good management?"

The answer to this is simply that such an attendance of irregulars *is* actually recognised in the class of which mention has been made. Every Sunday there are some present, invited often by the members themselves, who are perfect strangers to the teacher, but who will probably remain such for a short time only. This *un*method is rendered methodical by a very simple expedient. Entering the name, popularly termed "*joining*," is regarded as a very definite transaction; and it is perfectly well known that, once this has been done, the teacher recognises a new and full relationship to the new member. Until they have thus "joined," those in a sort of uncovenanted relationship to the class will not be invited to the annual or bi-annual festival, will not receive the much looked-for New Year's letter, and will only be regarded as friends, cordially welcome, but not *of* the class. "So and so can't *join*, for she is only to be in the place for a few weeks," is frequently a form of introduction to the teacher, when the class is over, and those wishing to give in their names are invited to stay back; "but I knew I might ask her, from you, while she's with us." It need hardly be added how cordially such apparently chance comers are welcome, while that they have been in reality no *chance* comers has been shown by the fact that from many thus attending letters have long after been received, in which, recalling themselves to the memory of the teacher, they have added that their introduction to a new life of faith and peace dated from that short Bible-class attendance, to all appearance casual and accidental.

A hymn—if possible prepared, and conducted in parts by a Bible-class choir—is the best opening. Those who have been detained by home duties, or the claims of service, to the last moment, are less shy of coming in late when every one is standing up and singing; and as, *except during prayers*, late comers can always steal into seats near the door left vacant to the last on purpose, the latest will probably have arrived before the short opening prayer for a blessing —the brief, earnest entreaty that the Master will be true to His promise, will not forsake His engagement to come down to meet those gathered together in His name.

The Scripture lesson should always be read by the teacher. The assurance that "no one is expected to read a word if they don't like," has brought many to attend a Bible-class who would never have entered the doors had there been a loop-hole for the possible display of "bad scholaring." Besides, educated reading, marked inflections of voice, and changes of tone and manner, will enable the hearers to grasp the meaning of the passage much more readily than if broken up into fragments by ten or twenty readers, each looking ahead for long words either for display or dreaded discomfiture.

And now comes the inquiry, "Would you ask questions, and expect answers, in an adult Bible-class?"

"Most certainly," we would reply: "questioning in and questioning out," is an essential to such teaching, if it is to be teaching actual and tangible. But let it be remembered that of all the departments of the work requiring skill and delicate handling the catechetical instruction of the adult class requires the most. It is well, in the arrangement of seats, to manage that, as far as possible, the young people freshly admitted from the Sunday-school should occupy the circle, one or two deep as the case may be, immediately fronting the teacher. They are accustomed to fearless answering, and will not be discouraged by an occasional mistake. Seeing that they answer and "come right," will probably induce others to venture a reply, when a general question is thrown out by the teacher. General questioning is bad in a Sunday-school, but often best in an adult class, where an individual question should never be asked unless the teacher is sure of the answerer. A public failure in answering a question will sometimes seal the lips of a member from that time forth, while the discovery that the right answer has been successfully given, with the cordial assent of both teacher and class, will start a hitherto silent listener on a career of interested and responsive attention, and, little by little, the habit of replying will spread from one to another. Many an answer, not sufficiently clear and defined to pass in a school class, should be accepted and placed in a favourable light by the teacher. Many a Bible-class attendant has not half the readiness and information of a regular Sunday-scholar, and comes with a mind dulled by hard work, and rusted by want of exercised faculties. The teacher should have tact and sympathy to feel with that particular hearer, and to present him with a first step out of a general chaos of thought in the form of a question in which he cannot help coming right.

The face and form of a certain Mrs. G—— come before us, who, week by week regular at a Bible-class, had invariably contented herself with the teacher's understood assurance that nobody should answer unless they liked, and had listened to the younger folks' eager replies without troubling herself further. The subject was from James v. 7—11, " Be patient therefore, brethren; ye have seen the end of the Lord," &c., and an illustration of the Lord's working out good by unlikely ways, and out of what we should call adverse circumstances, was drawn from a little child watching its mother making bread. The illustration was a homely one; but all the servants and mothers in the room were keenly alive to its appropriateness, as the teacher described the child thinking its mother must be making a mistake in preparing the dough, so unlike light and well-risen bread, in using salt, bitter yeast, the burning oven, &c., and Mrs. G——'s face showed her interest.

"And then what comes next—the salt or the yeast?" inquired the teacher, as she described the process. " Mrs. G——, don't let me make a mistake."

" The salt, ma'am—the salt next," eagerly interposed Mrs. G——, modestly conscious that, " come to bread, she *could* tell what was what," and who, from that day, was seldom shy of replying to a question.

We remember a rough country lass who, having been sent by her mistress to a Bible-class, listened for some time with an open-mouthed stare to all that went forward. For one or two weeks she came, always in a species of full-blown amazement, as she hurried from the kitchen fire, a mass of unkempt hair blown up round her face, her bonnet falling back, and her eyes showing ever new astonishment as she found, from the kind reception by all in the class, that she was expected and welcome, and, still more, that religion seemed to have something in it for her—something that she could understand, and that might go into her own rough kitchen life. No individual question had ever been addressed to her; as a failure would have been more than probable, and the rough girl was shy and sensitive. But one day, as the description was being given of the two disciples being sent into Jerusalem to prepare the paschal supper, and as, from previous instruction, the teacher prepared to ask concerning the lamb which they would have to make ready, she inquired, "And now, what would St. Peter and St. John have to do first?"

"Cotch it!" was the eager reply of the poor girl, who for the first time plunged into the subject, and who looked in an instant shyer than before, as the impulse furnished, probably, by a reminiscence from her country village, prompted her to answer.

Nothing but the most determined gravity on the part of the teacher would have checked the smile rising into a laugh on the faces of some of the younger ones. But Ellen was quite reassured by the answer: "Quite right, Ellen: nothing could be done until they had got the lamb, and to get it was the first thing; only, as spotless lambs had been already set aside for sacrifice, they would have been able to get it without much trouble."

From that hour Ellen was an eager listener, and, when she was pretty sure of coming right, an answerer also. The next time, the subject having been resumed previously to entering on the fulfilled type, the question was asked, "And what did we notice last time that they were to be very careful about in preparing the lamb for roasting?"

There was hardly time for the question, before Ellen's round face kindled into an "I remember" expression, as she put in, "Warn't to splinter not a bone of it;" and was radiant when a "Quite right" confirmed her as a successful answerer.

There are two or three sorts of questioning which should be successively used in a Bible-class—the first almost infantine in its simplicity, but which will lead on successfully to the next: What do we call this parable? What do we mean by prodigal? How many sons had the father? What do we know of the country to which the youngest went? &c. As in lighting a fire, the paper first catches the flame, which then spreads to stronger material, so this easy questioning will lead on to inquiries needing more thoughtful answers: What are these three parables intended to teach? What sorts of people were listening to Jesus as he spoke to them? Can you see a difference between the two first parables and the last? In the two first we have a picture of the finder seeking what was lost; but what do we have in the third? And then will follow from the answer, "The lost one seeking to be restored," the earnest appeal in which the hearers have the great love of the Father brought before them, the welcome to heart and home set forth as for themselves.

Before, however, leaving the subject of questioning, it should be observed that, as a matter of course, this process will begin with questions as to the lesson of the previous Sunday. "Taking up the stitches" is too important a process ever to be neglected; and much would be lost to absentees from the preceding lesson, and to many with short memories, were the teacher to omit doing it at the very first, thus starting the new subject from foregone instructions.

The last twenty minutes of the Bible-class lesson should be, to our thinking, wholly dedicated to an address and connected exposition from the teacher, who will have furnished himself with anecdote, illustration, and explanatory store during the week's preparation. How earnest, how loving, how pleading, how solemn, this concluding portion of the teaching should be, can be felt only by those who have themselves realised how solemn a thing it is to live, how solemn a thing to die, and who are vividly conscious that to his hearers the Gospel must come as a matter of life and death.

Some clear-pointed lesson, some earnest thought definitely to be carried away—" to be put under the pillow at night and taken out in the morning"—should always be left with the hearers. A plan found very helpful and uniting in one Bible-class, is that of taking a motto for the week, which teacher and hearers agree to adopt, and with which they frequently greet each other when meeting out of doors or in private—a sort of password, giving a sense of union and of enlistment in the same company. Such mottoes have from time to time been—" *Unto the Lord;*" "*Looking unto Jesus;*" "*My help cometh from the Lord;*" "*We serve the Lord Christ;*" "*We seek a city;*" "*He liveth for evermore;*" "*The Lord is risen;*" "*I also overcame;*" "*Walk worthy of the Lord,*" &c.

The choice of the closing hymn will often give the teacher the opportunity of showing a little individual remembrance of the circumstances of one or another of the class. " William, you will be far away next Sunday: you must choose our hymn for us to-day, that we may remember which was your favourite." " Mary, this is the first time you have been able to come since your illness: you must choose the hymn this afternoon;"

and if William or Mary are shy or embarrassed, in a moment they will be put at their ease, and gratified also, by the suggestion—" I think you like this one, do you not ? Would you like us to sing this ?"

The closing prayer will sum up the subject of the lesson, and in it, ere its conclusion, the teacher will remember the sick and absent members of the class, those in special need, Confirmation candidates, &c.

It is well to have it understood that he remains behind for entering names, inquiries after sick or absent members, and for the various small transactions generally needing attention at the conclusion of the proceedings.

Where there are long-tried and earnest Christian members in a Bible-class, a short after-meeting of about ten minutes, in which they will themselves unite with the teacher in prayer for each other and for the class, will be found a most uniting and powerful means of usefulness and progress. It has been truly said, " Good prayers never come weeping home."

Opening or Closing Hymn

For Sunday Schools, Teacher's Meetings, Adult Bible Classes, &c.

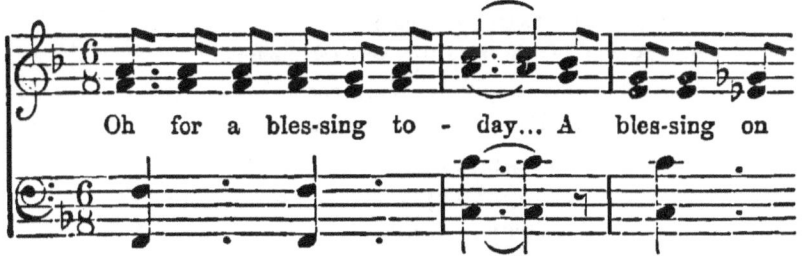

Oh for a bles-sing to - day... A bles-sing on

Oh, for a blessing to-day!
  A blessing on all we may hear; }
        [or; have heard;]
Jesus, be with us, we pray,
  In Spirit and power draw near.
        [or, And order our steps in Thy word.]

Sin and transgression we bring,
  Unburdening our load at Thy feet;
Only for pardon we cling
  To Him at whose promise we meet.

Hungry and thirsty, we flee
  To One who restoreth the soul:
Seeking our refuge in Thee,
  Thou Saviour who makest us whole.

Oh, for a message of peace!
  A word from Thy lips to each heart;
Doubts and misgivings shall cease
  If Jesus His presence impart.

Oh, for a blessing to-day!
  Since, Lord, at Thy word we have come;
Send us not empty away,
  E'en now let each heart be Thy home!

CHAPTER V.

THE HOUR SET APART.

THE Sunday instruction is by no means the limit of the teacher's duties and responsibilities. On the contrary, it will be increasingly found that the work ramifies into channels of thought and sympathy so numerous and varied, that the head of a large Bible-class will realise, as years go on, that, to carry out his work thoroughly and effectively, he must regard it as a distinctive calling, involving many an hour of week-day labour and correspondence, and a dedication to the Master's service of much which will by no means cost him nothing.

The periodical visitation of its members will, of course, be regarded as a necessary corollary to the Bible-class teaching, the subject then discussed forming often the topic of more close and personal conversation than is possible on the Sunday. The individual knowledge thus gained by the teacher, of the homes and occupations of those by whom he weekly finds himself surrounded, will enable him to fashion the Sunday's lesson with special reference to their needs, trials, and difficulties, so that the bow shall seldom be drawn at a venture.

It would be almost superfluous to write in this place concerning visits to sick members, efforts to find suitable situations for those who may be out of place, or concerning the unwearied remembrance of little, as well as great, needs, which should carry the conviction to each member of the class that "my teacher never forgets." All these go to strengthen and deepen the work that we seek to render work for eternity. It is rather of those who cannot be visited in their own homes—of those in service who would be unable to receive their teacher in their master's house, or among other servants—of those in business who are at their trade and in the workshop, behind the counter, or at the sewing-machine, from morning till night, that we would now speak; of those who, separated from their own homes, and busy amongst strangers in their daily employments, need, even more than they otherwise might, the sympathy, personal intimacy, guidance, and counsel, of an earnest teacher.

On behalf of such attendants at the Bible-class we would advocate the adoption of a plan which has been found to command results of no small importance—that of an hour being set apart by teachers, during which they shall at their own houses be accessible, and, yet more, avowedly awaiting visits from its members: an hour when the door shall stand open to them and to them only, and which they may be led to regard as their property as entirely as that devoted to the Sunday instruction in the class-room.

The effective working of this arrangement will probably require some self-denial on the part of the teacher, as it will most certainly call for tact, delicacy, and peculiar powers of setting shy visitors at their ease; but the hour thus devoted may bring an interest of results which—and these words are written from a conviction following long experience of the plan— eternity alone will reveal. To this may and should belong that close, heart-to-heart intercourse which in many an instance has led, by God's blessing, to life-long decision for Christ.

The time thus set apart should, if possible, be in the evening. Practically, no other would be available for servants, or for young persons in business. Some prudent reader may be inclined to say : " Will not inviting young people to come through the streets in the evening lead to mischief?" And our answer is, " Will it not be better that they should come to the house of their teacher, to meet the kind welcome, the earnest sympathy, the help upwards, of a true friend, than that they should find their way to other friends less sure, or go to other houses less helpful ?" It is their only spare time ; and the very willingness to overcome the shyness attendant on a first visit, at least, to their superior in station, is an evidence of such a desire after something higher and better than the surroundings of their ordinary life, as will almost certainly keep them from abusing the opportunity thus given.

It may be well to say publicly in the Bible-class, " I wish all the friends here to remember that I am at home in the evenings from half-past seven to nine (it may be) to any who may like to come and see me. I hope all who wish to do so *will* come. There are many little difficulties which one or another of you may have, and of which we could not talk before others, in which, perhaps, you might be helped, if we were to be alone together. Besides, I find I can make friends better with each one after a chat in my own room." Pleasant words like these, with a smile of anticipatory welcome, will encourage many a member of the Bible-class who has longed for such an invitation, to take advantage of it ; and probably it will not be long before the familiar announcement of " a young person wishing to speak to you," will be heard, while the teacher, as the specified hour approaches, wonders as to whether the invitation will be accepted.

And now as to the conduct of such interviews.

At the very outset, we would venture to say to every teacher not as yet at home in such a plan, Remember your own feelings at the very shyest moment of your life. Try and recall what you felt when you were very young, and went on your first visit from home; or when you had to make your first call by yourself, and were asking yourself, all along the passages, what you should say to account for your appearance. And then multiply all those sensations as much as you please, if you would realise to yourself the feelings of embarrassment against which, very probably, your evening visitor is struggling in answer to your invitation.

In the first place, see that your servant is prepared to open the door to an *expected* guest who is to be made immediately welcome. It goes a long way to quiet Jane's anxieties, after ringing the bell, if she is met by the maid with a kindly welcome, with a cordial " Come in; Miss A. will be so glad to see you; she was saying she hoped some of the class would be coming to see her this evening:" and while she is thinking to herself in the passage how she may best excuse herself, now that she is fairly launched upon her visit, a sense of being expected will at once begin to reassure her.

It need hardly be said that, as a matter of course, she will find herself alone with her teacher. No one with the least comprehension of the delicacy and the importance of visits such as these, would dream of subjecting a shy visitor to the confusion of finding herself unexpectedly called to account for her appearance before others; nor should she have to do this in any case. No greater mistake could be made than to meet a member of the Bible-class who has been induced to make the effort of coming on her own account for help and sympathy, with the greeting, however kindly meant, "Did you wish to speak to me?" "What is it that you wished to say to me?" Such a form of accosting our visitor, throwing the onus of the undertaking immediately upon her, would, in all probability, seal her lips. Rather should the teacher at once assume and maintain it. "I am so glad you have come to pay me a visit in my own little room, Jane! I was hoping you would, for almost all my friends know it, and I like my Bible-class friends to know their way to it always. Isn't it pleasant and snug?"

Jane shyly, but much relieved that her teacher's apartment, and not her reason for seeking it, has come first under discussion, says that "it do seem very quiet and pleasant."

"And I must show you my pictures, Jane; I hope you are fond of photographs, for some of these are great favourites of mine." And the teacher will, perhaps, take her candle and point out some of those hanging on the walls, telling their stories in a few words to her visitor, who begins to feel increasingly at her ease.

"This is a picture of Mr. E., our clergyman. Isn't it a good likeness? And this is where we used to live. Look here at that little garden-walk, and at that arbour, or at those woods on the hill. That was my favourite walk," and so on.

And after a time the pictures, and the little glimpses into her teacher's own life—the confidence, perhaps, as to those woods having been a place of meeting with a Saviour's love, or as to that arbour having been associated with happy readings of other days, or as to that little photographed grave being the resting-place of some dear brother or sister, "not lost, but gone before"—will bring to the visitor's mind the conviction, more felt than realised, that after all she and teacher are at one about some sorts of things: Miss A. had an old home which she cared for, and so had she; and likes photographs, and so does she; and by-and-by, when the pictures have come to an end, and when the question naturally seems to follow, " And now I should so much like to know about *your* home before you went out to service—was it in the country? Are your parents there still? Have you any picture of it or of them, for if you have, I hope you will let me see them one day;"—by-and-by, and when her tongue has been thus unloosed, she will find herself talking more freely than she had ever thought to speak to one whom she had before known comparatively at a distance; and the description, helped out by a few kind questions, of her village Sunday-school, her country home, and the number and callings of brothers and sisters, will furnish a series of confidences the very utterance of which will pave the way to that union and interchange of sympathy which should belong to the close relationship of the teacher and the taught.

And then after a time those confidences will take a deeper tone: "It is a great pleasure to me to see you at the Bible-class on Sundays, Jane; I am sure you must try very hard, to be able to attend regularly." And Jane, it may be, answers that "she'd try harder still, rather than miss; that it do seem more home-like, and more kind of for helping one through one's work, every time you go." And then will follow the earnest inquiry, "And how is it with you, dear sister? Could *you* feel that you knew something of what we were speaking of last Sunday, of the peace which belongs to those who have found Jesus—who have heard Him say, Thy sins are forgiven thee? Have *you* felt that sin-burden—that something between you and Him which I knew, too, until I laid my sins on Him, and took Him at His word, and was made whole?"

We will not go further; Jane is no longer thinking what she shall say, or whether her teacher will think her "taking a liberty" in coming. She has felt the power of true, loving, earnest sympathy, and her story is told—the feeling that she has "tried the best she could, and don't seem to get right;" that "ever since that day at the Bible-class when you spoke about our building on the rock, and not on the sand," she has been wanting to get hold of Jesus, and to build upon what He did for her; but her prayers "don't seem to get no higher than the ceiling," and she "don't seem to get any sure hopes." And the teacher's work is before her—to help a sister soul straight to the Lord—to show her, by the most simple illustrations, the meaning of Christ's substitution in the sinner's stead, the necessity of taking Him completely at His word, the simplicity of that transaction which yet is the one transaction for eternity, the laying the sins upon Him, the receiving the pardon, invisible but sure, from a real living Saviour, invisible and very sure; and after a while the two are together before Him, kneeling hand in hand in His presence, pleading His love, bringing the cause of the weary-hearted to Him who was Himself weary; and the hour set apart has not been in vain.

"It was my birthday night," said to her teacher one thus brought to the Lord, and afterwards called to years of active service in the missionary field—" it was my birthday night, that dark December night when I felt so ashamed to come and see you, and yet I did come; and you said you was so glad to see me; and you showed me all that was meant in those words, 'the Lord hath laid on Him the iniquity of us all,' and I took Him at His word and believed it was for me, and came to Him, and He pardoned me. I never forget the day when it comes round."

It will be well to have in store a supply of leaflets, cards, little books—all attractive in appearance—constituting short and impressive memorials of visits such as I have been describing, and perpetuating their influence. There are few teachers who will not for themselves have made a selection of those best suited to the purpose.

Youths are shyer than young women in coming to the houses of their teachers; and Bible-class teachers of both sexes will often find it expedient to invent some device for giving to members of their classes a definite pretext for a visit such as we have described. It has been found a good plan, for instance, at some annual distribution of books, such as may have taken place at Christmas or the New Year, to say to the class, "I have not written any names in the books, because I want you to bring them to me that I may have the pleasure of a visit from you when I do so." The receivers will, probably, feel their presents incomplete until the names are written in the books, and will feel it in a sense due to the giver to bring them; and the teacher should know how to improve the opportunity to such advantage as to make the evening visitors anxious to repeat the call. To find themselves received as respected and welcome guests, treated with delicate consideration, admitted to the confidence of their teacher as a true friend, and thanked, at shaking hands on parting, for their visits, will be to find themselves raised in their own self-respect, and, in many cases—more than will ever be known here—helped to the Friendship, of which all earthly friendship is but a type, the Fellowship which is with the Father, and with His Son Jesus Christ, for those who have realised in their own experience that the blood of Jesus Christ cleanseth us from all sin.

The writer cannot close this paper without a word of apology to very many who may justly regard themselves as abundantly capable of conducting interviews with the members of their Bible-classes, without any necessity for hints such as have here been offered. The excuse which must be pleaded is the frequency with which, in the advocacy of the plan forming the subject of this paper, the objection has been offered by really earnest teachers—" But, if they came to see me, I should feel shy; I shouldn't know what to say to them—I should not think of questions which would help them to tell me about themselves." If to any such the suggestions here offered may prove of service, leading them to a stronger sense of the importance of this department of Bible-class work, and of the hold which may be gained on individual members by its faithful administration, their object will have been abundantly attained. The setting apart of a fixed time, the dedication of an hour, evening by evening, to the guidance, help, teaching, cheering, building up of those for whom we shall have hereafter to give account, may and will, in all probability, involve a real sacrifice and self-denial on the part of the teacher, especially if it should come at the close of a day already engrossed by anxious and laborious occupation. But the seed thus sown will be reaped hereafter. The hour thus set apart here may, "on the other side," and to that other soul, mean ETERNITY.

CHAPTER VI.

ON PREPARATION FOR ADULT BAPTISM.

To this and the following papers a few prefatory words should be affixed. It might seem, at first sight, as if, in dwelling successively on preparation for three of our most important Church ordinances, the writer were in some sort attributing to the Bible-class teacher responsibilities more properly belonging to the clergyman. For admission to each one of these the final responsibility rests, of course, with the latter; and, in many instances, in some small and country parishes, for example, the whole course of preparation is assumed and carried on by him alone. But, in a large number of cases, as the readers of these chapters are well aware, minute, individual preparation of candidates by their ministers is an absolute impossibility. Where the population is numbered by thousands, and the candidates are reckoned by scores, class preparation alone, supplemented, it may be, by a single private interview, is all that can possibly be given even by the most earnest and laborious pastor; and, in many cases, candidates of the humbler class, young persons in service, lads and young women in shops or mills, are prevented from availing themselves of pastoral instruction, which would otherwise be within their reach, by the clashing of hours and the restrictions of their respective callings. In many such cases the real preparation, so far as it lies with any human instrument, must practically fall on the teacher, provided that such teacher be willing to throw himself heart and soul into the work; and there are few earnest and conscientious clergymen, struggling against the overwhelming sense of work which cannot be overtaken, who do not know the relief of mind belonging to the reception of candidates carefully prepared by laborious and thorough-going teachers; the inward exclamation—" Mr. A.'s lads; I shall find them already instructed!" "Miss L.'s Bible-class candidates! the hard work will have been done for me. She is sure to have given herself to their preparation!" and there are few, probably, who have not uttered the wish that other candidates, possibly of higher position, might be so cared for.

And it is of this preparation that we would write—this conscientious, detailed teaching which should never take anything for granted, which should break up the fallow ground of ignorance, root up weeds of prejudice, never be satisfied by anything short of thorough comprehension, or of a deposition on the very "ground of the heart" of those truths which the Holy Spirit's influence must water and cause to spring forth unto life everlasting. Few clergymen have time individually to penetrate the ignorance which the teacher must meet, and, little by little, must clear away; and it is in this view of his duties that the following suggestions are offered concerning preparation for Baptism, Confirmation, and the Lord's Supper.

From a large and carefully taught Bible-class candidates for Baptism will be continually presenting themselves. Some whose parents are Baptists, and others who have been so neglected as never to have been admitted into Church-fellowship, will, from time to time, be bringing to their teachers the request for admission to this Sacrament; and, need it be added that, of all the rites of the Christian religion, it is generally in that class the one least understood.

Assuming the candidate to have been already instructed in the history of man's fall, our Lord's life, and other needful truths, the question which, after a brief preparatory conversation, must introduce the subject, will be the inquiry of the teacher—"And now, tell me *why* you wish to be baptized?" This will, as a general rule, be but vaguely answered. "I think people ought to be baptized;" "Because it's in the Bible;" and even the simple "Jesus Christ said so," are replies frequently given, with a general well-meaningness which is far removed from clear comprehension. And, as the subject is one which involves a laying down before the inquirers consecutively and at length of the whole scheme, so to speak, of Christian doctrine, the teacher should, indeed, take heed to it that his own preparation be thorough and prayerful; that he come to his Bible with no prejudiced views, but be himself an earnest learner, seeking more and more to know the Master's will concerning this, His ordained rite.

Leaving, for the present, the question of Infant Baptism, which, however, we believe to be both right and Scriptural, we proceed to the first step in the instruction of the adult candidate—that, namely, of dwelling with all force and earnestness on *our lost condition by nature.* (See Pref. to Bapt. Service.) The very fact of inquiry and diligence as to salvation will probably reveal a sense of sin and of need on the part of the inquirer; and the teacher will know how to describe those convictions of sin, that sense of "something wrong between me and God," that lying awake at night with the thought, "Suppose I were to die!" that uneasiness underlying church attendance, saying of prayers, reading of chapters, which belongs to an awakened, but as yet unsatisfied soul; so that, just as hope comes to the sick man who hears his own symptoms, doubted and disregarded by others, detailed from previous knowledge by a physician able to discern and powerful to heal—the listener, who could hardly himself have put into words his longings, fears, yearnings, and uneasiness, will kindle into an almost surprised attention at the proof that his teacher "seems to know everything about what he feels like."

"It's just that exactly," will be probably his expressed or unexpressed ejaculation; "and one seems always to be on the other side from people who are good, and sure of going to heaven."

"And now tell me, dear friend, if you, who say that you are unhappy about your sinfulness, long for something better—long to give yourself to a really new life—not to be a mere church-goer or outside Christian, but to have all the happiness which comes from being wholly Jesus Christ's servant." And it will be the heartfelt "Yes" of the hearer which will be the foundation of the teacher's instruction and course of preparation.

The next step will be to prove to the learner the existence—now,—here,—at this very time,—of two completely distinct conditions, as distinct and separate from each other as a resurrection-life divided from the former life by death—as the services of different masters—as a wife's in her marriage to successive husbands: the references, of course, being to the three comparisons in Rom. vi. and vii., ushered in by the "Know ye not?" of the Apostle.

In order to prevent confusion of metaphor, it will be well to dwell chiefly on the first. The state is supposed of a criminal so wholly sunk in sin as at last to be condemned to death. The justice of the condemnation is pointed out; the impossibility of the judge's passing over the crime consistently with being a just judge; the necessity for the vindication of a righteous law. Then let there follow the supposition of such a criminal's suffering the penalty of death, of his actually being submerged, of his life actually passing away under the river's tide, and of his guilt being met by the last and extreme punishment of the law. The hearer will then be led to imagine a practically impossible case—the case (as pictured forth in the dual type of Lev. xiv.) of another distinct life being given to that person—a life not burdened with the guilt, not under the threatened penalty of a broken law, as was the former life—the case of a second life divided from the first by death and burial, a life, if the owner so choose, to be dedicated to new purposes and new aims.

It may take many words to bring such a picture before the scholar; but it must be done; and it must be done laboriously and patiently, if the foundation is to be laid for clear and distinct teaching concerning the ordinance which, with a force and distinctness for which we can never enough thank Him who consecrated it for us, shows forth the Christian's standpoint and position when washed, justified, and sanctified.

And in this place it may be necessary to remind the teacher that *Baptism by immersion* is the form of Baptism which furnishes the key to the teaching of the New Testament upon the subject; that the image must be exactly and vividly presented to the mind, in order to a full understanding of the force of the type wherein death, burial, and resurrection are evidently set forth. Such Baptism is rubrically directed by the Church of England (see Baptismal Services); baptism by sprinkling, or rather by " pouring water," being the authorised alternative ordinarily demanded by our climate, and ordinarily adopted as a matter of convenience. And although the form in which the rite is administered be comparatively of small moment, although the "sprinkling" of the Old Testament ritual (Numb. viii. 7; xix. 13, &c.) showed forth cleansing and expunging of past uncleanness as truly as would immersion have shown it forth, and the beautiful prophetic promise, " I will sprinkle clean water upon you and ye shall be clean," stood as the symbolic expression interpreted by the further promise, " From all your filthiness and from all your idols will I cleanse you"; still, and for the full comprehension of what Baptism signifies, *the passing under the water* must be clearly and vividly presented to the mind as that which gives the clue to the meaning of the Christ-ordained ritual.

The teacher will now dwell with far more force, and more at length than is possible in a sketch like the present, upon the condition under sentence of death in which we stand by nature, and upon its utter depravity and guilt. "The soul that sinneth it shall die!" That is God's sentence. He cannot pass it over. The curse of sin, the doom of death, is upon the sinner; and it is the sense of this sin, the feeling that you are exposed to God's just anger, which makes you now afraid to die. If that were taken off you, would you not have peace?"

And then will follow a setting forth of Christ as the Substitute of the sinner. It was necessary that He should become man to bear the curse of man. He took not upon Him the nature of angels, but He took on Him the seed of Abraham. "Forasmuch then as the children are partakers of flesh and blood, He also Himself likewise took part of the same, that through death He might destroy Him that had the power of death, that is, the devil; and deliver them who through fear of death were all their lifetime subject to bondage." As man's Substitute He died, having borne the whole curse, the whole punishment, in our stead. The cry, "My God, my God, why hast Thou forsaken Me?" was for us. "He was made," or accounted, "sin for us." "Thy reproach hath broken My heart," was for us. "He was wounded for our transgressions, bruised for our iniquities; all we like sheep have gone astray, but the Lord hath laid on Him the iniquity of us all."

And thus came to pass the baptism that He was baptized with; the death, and the leaving all the imputed sin, even as the grave-clothes in the sepulchre, on this side of the grave; the immersion, so to speak, under the ground in burial; the resurrection to a new life, and to a glorified existence, and the ascension to the right hand of the Father until He shall appear the second time without sin unto salvation. And so he who comes to Christ, who takes Him at His word, who casts on Him his sin, who, by the Holy Spirit, is enabled to lay hold of Him as a Saviour, is regarded as having actually died for his own sin, and as having borne the penalty of the law in the person of His proxy; as having been buried when Christ was buried, the whole guilt and the whole punishment having been left on the other side of the grave; as having risen and ascended in His person, and as now, even now, by Him our Representative, sitting in heavenly places in the court of heaven.

This is, so to speak, the forensic, or court of justice meaning of Baptism. It represents the position of the believer as regarded by the Father who gave His Son for his salvation. "I through the law am dead to the law"—or dead by the execution of the law upon my Substitute, and am reckoned to be "dead indeed unto sin, but alive unto God through Jesus Christ our Lord." "I am crucified with Christ." "Buried with Him in baptism;" "nevertheless I live, yet not I, but Christ liveth in me." "Wherein also we are risen with Him." "Old things are passed away, all things are become new." We are in the resurrection-life; separated from the former by death and burial. "If ye then be risen with Christ, seek those things which are above, where Christ sitteth at the right hand of God. For ye are dead, and your life is hid with Christ in God."

The histories of Noah and of Israel, introduced in the beautiful opening prayer of our Baptismal Service, to each of which belonged a former abode in sin or bondage, a leaving behind of that former life, immersion, as a more completely significant type of death and burial to that former life, and a starting upon an entirely fresh existence, dissevered from all that had gone before, will forcibly illustrate these points; and in Rom. vi. 1—6 a full view of the position represented by Baptism is given.

And here will follow what we may term the *second*

part of the teaching of Baptism, summed up for us with admirable force and power in our Baptismal Service: "Baptism doth represent unto us our profession, which is, to follow the example of our Saviour Christ, and to be made like unto Him; that as He died and rose again for us, so should we who are baptized die from sin and rise again unto righteousness."

There is a sure, certain, though unseen connection over which presides the Lord and Giver of life, between the fact of our taking hold of Christ as our Substitute and accepting His work in our stead,—between this transaction carried forward in our secret intercourse with our great Representative, and that of our actually dying to the power of sin as a master, and to the dominion of Satan in our hearts, and, as it were, passing up from the burial of our old nature, which was contrary to Christ, to a new life. "That they which live should not henceforth live unto themselves, but unto Him who died for them and rose again."

The Epistles abound with statements concerning this doctrine. It is often the thread glistening and shining to the surface upon which whole chapters of thought and teaching are strung; and the teacher, desirous of guidance into all truth, will do well to prepare himself for the teaching of others by tracing it out through lines of argument such as belong, for instance, to the Epistles to the Romans, Ephesians, and

Colossians. He will observe how the forensic or judicial position of the believer is set forth—the being *reckoned* dead unto sin through having paid its penalty by proxy, as brought out in some verses, for example, of Rom. vi., being indissolubly intertwined with a showing forth of the moral or spiritual change which belongs to the true taking hold of the Substitute. "That henceforth we should not serve sin." "Let not sin, therefore, reign in your mortal bodies that ye should obey it in the lusts thereof; neither yield ye your members as instruments of unrighteousness unto sin; but yield yourselves unto God *as those that are alive from the dead.*"

The same view of the necessity of death to sin and a new life unto holiness, by the faith of the Son of God, is carried out in St. Paul's illustration of a change of masters; and this comparison will often prove a very forcible one if well used by the teacher. It begins with Rom. vi. 16, and ends with the summary, "Being now made free from sin and become servants to God, ye have your fruit unto holiness, and the end everlasting life." "The wages of sin is death; but the gift of God is eternal life through Jesus Christ our Lord."

The same truth is illustrated in the seventh chapter, by the case of a woman bound to a first husband, being by death made free from his bondage, and married to another. So the soul, made free from its union with sin and the world, is ready to be united, "married to another, even to Him who is raised from the dead, *that we should bring forth fruit unto God.*"*

His complete change of condition who has thus left behind him allegiance to sin and Satan, and who has, by the power of the Holy Spirit, been united to the dying and risen Substitute, is powerfully brought out in Col. ii. 12 and the following verses. For instance, "If ye be dead with Christ from the elements of the world—why, *as though living in the world*"—a world left behind for ever, as completely as if you had died and had a second distinct life given to you—"are ye subject to ordinances?" And the thought expressed in the beautiful Easter Even Collect—the eve on which our great Representative was immersed under the earth, and lay buried, to rise on the morrow— "Grant that as we are baptized into the death of thy blessed Son our Saviour Jesus Christ, so by continually mortifying our corrupt affections, we may be buried with Him," is carried on in the deep teaching of the Easter Epistle, "If ye then be risen with Christ, seek those things which are above; for ye are dead, and your life is hid with Christ in God." And the setting

* Every student of this subject should, if possible, study closely Chalmers' Lectures on the Romans, particularly on Rom. iv. and vi.

of the affections of the risen life on the ascended Saviour is with equal force and beauty made the substance of the Ascension-day Prayer :—

Grant, we beseech Thee, Almighty God, that like as we do believe Thy only-begotten Son, our Lord Jesus Christ, to have ascended into the heavens ; so we may also in heart and mind thither ascend, and with Him continually dwell, who liveth and reigneth with Thee and the Holy Ghost, one God, world without end. *Amen.*

So also in the Baptismal Service the prayer is made :—

"O merciful God, grant that the old Adam in these persons may be so buried that the new man may be raised up in them.

"Grant that all carnal affections may die in them, and that all things belonging to the Spirit may live and grow in them."

And it will be at this point that the teacher will be led to dwell on the struggle after holiness, the walk as becometh saints, the heaven-set affections which must belong to the risen life—the new life of faith in the Son of God. There are still "members which are upon the earth." Though passed from death unto life, though having gone through the transition from Satan's kingdom to Christ's kingdom in the act of union to the sacrificed Saviour, we are still in the body of death—have still the law of sin in our members, which have not yet been subjected to the bodily death from which they will arise purified for ever. Though the will be now for ever on Christ's side, the flesh wars still against the spirit. But we are enlisted into

His ranks who can make us more than conquerors. The soldier may be in the enemy's camp, but he is the King's soldier now. The seed may be planted in an unfriendly soil, but it is the seed of God—His husbandry, to flourish by-and-by in the courts of the house of our God.

And oh, how much will the teacher himself gain by throwing his heart fully and unreservedly into the views to which the study of this subject introduces him! Let him read the 6th, 7th, and 8th chapters of the Romans, without a break,—passing from the actual transition from death to life shown forth in Baptism, and described in the 6th chapter, to the struggle pourtrayed in the 7th; and then going on to the 8th, "beginning with no condemnation and ending with no separation," which tells of the present assured safety of him that is in Christ Jesus, walking not after the flesh but after the Spirit, heir of God, joint-heir with Christ, having suffered in and with Him—called, justified, sanctified, and yet to be glorified: let the teacher, we repeat, ponder, study, pray over these truths, and from a full heart, and from his own standing-point on Christ's side of the grave, he will be able with love and power to bring them home to his hearer.

After what has been written, it will be hardly needful to impress upon the teacher, who, be it remembered, is dealing with *adults*, the importance of earnestly impressing his hearers with the truth that the real Baptism—the repentance for the past, and the faith—the actual taking hold for himself of Jesus as a perfect Sacrifice and Substitute—the repentance and faith spoken of in the Catechism, and which are the work of the Holy Spirit in the heart of the sinner, must *precede* the showing forth of the death unto sin and the new birth unto righteousness, in the sacred and beautiful outward rite. "For *by one Spirit are we all baptized into one body*" (1 Cor. xii. 13). It was when the real Baptism had taken place in the eunuch's heart, when he had seen Christ as the Lamb "led to the slaughter," and had grasped the sacrifice with the hand of faith, that he was baptized. Philip said, "If thou believest with all thine heart, thou mayest." And he believed, and showed forth his profession, and went on his way rejoicing. No better subject than this history can be selected by the teacher for one of his preparation lessons, and for showing the necessity of a previous condition of living faith in a crucified Saviour.

And these views do not lower the dignity of our Christ-ordained Sacrament. Rather do they raise and elevate it. Although the soldier enrolled in the army must have already given his heart and determined to devote his life to the service of the King, the enlistment into the ranks and his public recognition as one of Christ's sworn cross-bearers is a happy and a joyful occasion. As the Twenty-seventh Article, which is an admirable exponent of the subject, reminds us, " The promises of forgiveness of sin, and of our adoption to be the sons of God by the Holy Ghost, are visibly signed and sealed; faith is confirmed, and grace increased by virtue of prayer unto God." Though already *in heart* one of the militant company carrying on the warfare in an enemy's land, it is no unmeaning privilege which admits him outwardly into their number. And the last look towards the shores of death, the farewell to the old bondage, the new *Christian* name, the sign of the cross on the brow, the glorious words of welcome into the congregation of Christ's flock, the oath of allegiance, consecrated as it has been by centuries, during which it has testified the determination of those who have stood to confess the faith of Christ crucified, and to fight manfully under His banner—all these constitute a transaction too real and too solemn to be lightly regarded. That the Lord of ordinances will not fail to be present when sought in His own ordinances we cannot doubt; and all that can be done by a teacher to make the Baptismal day one of deep and solemn interest should be done unsparingly. He will of course be the witness, the earnest, prayerful witness, at the font—the first to give the hand of welcome to the newly-admitted brother, anp to make him feel that the brotherhood of Baptism is true and real. And, probably, the evening of the day will see both teacher and learner once more at the footstool of the great Ordainer of the baptismal rite, seeking for help, strength, teaching, guidance for the new resurrection life.

But this chapter has exceeded the bounds assigned. It may be that the writer has been led, from the very sense of all that it should convey of help and assurance, to enlarge upon the subject too much at length. It is, however, with the earnest hope that some brother or sister teachers may be led, for themselves in the first place, and, in the next, for their hearers, to seek for God's Holy Spirit's teaching on His Word concerning Baptism, that it has been thus considered. It may possibly arouse the question in some hearts, "Have I been as yet baptized by the Holy Ghost?" "Has that washing away of sin by the blood of Christ, which the water of baptism 'mystically' shows forth, really taken place in my heart?" "Does my life show that the death unto sin and the new birth unto righteousness have taken place in me?" "Am I living a risen life in Christ Jesus?"

And then the need of a present, living, powerful Spirit will be realised. Oh, that from all of us who have taken to ourselves the office of teachers of His Word, the prayer may continually arise—

Grant, O Lord, that as we are baptized into the death of Thy blessed Son, our Saviour Jesus Christ, so by continual mortifying our corrupt affections we may be buried with him; and that through the grave, the gate of death, we may pass to our joyful resurrection; for His merits, who died and was buried, and rose again for us, Thy Son Jesus Christ our Lord. *Amen.*

And let those of us who *have* passed from death unto life seek to walk as those that are alive from the dead, and remember that "as many of us as have been baptized into Christ have put on Christ"—that from the Baptism of the Holy Spirit, whether it precede, as it should do, or whether it follow or accompany adult Baptism, believers arise *covered over in Christ* to the greeting of the New Covenant, "Ye are My sons and My daughters, saith the Lord Almighty."

PREPARATION LESSONS FOR CANDIDATES.*

For the assistance of teachers who may be preparing candidates for Baptism, and whose time may be so engaged as to make it desirable to consult notes already furnished, the following sketches of lessons have been prepared. It will be found that they include the explanation of the Service for Adult Baptism, passages from which are marked in italics:—

I.
WHERE WE STAND BY NATURE.

Preface to Baptismal Service. "Conceived and born in sin." Doom of sinners. Sense of sin separating from God. There must be a change of condition for salvation. STORY OF NICODEMUS (*Gospel in Baptismal Service*). He wanted to know how he could get into a new life. Jesus said, John iii. 3; explained it by verse 5. Should be translated, "Except a man be born of water and spirit, or *breath*" (the same word being used by our Lord which denotes in Greek or Hebrew, wind or breath). N. ought to have known this. "Art thou the teacher of Israel and knowest not?" How? He would have known if he had remembered Ezekiel's prophecy. Water, Ezek. xxxvi. 26. Breath or wind, Ezek. xxxvii. If we are to be saved, we must be washed and cleansed from sin. WATER indicates CLEANSING; in Levitical ritual signified BLOOD OF CHRIST, Numb. viii. 7, xix. 9; Heb. ix. 10, 14, x. 4, 22. Spirit or breath indicates *quickening*. Holy Spirit, John iii. 8. So Jesus repeated in other words the old prophecy of Ezekiel, to one who professed to teach the prophets. Promise attached in Ezekiel, "Ye shall be my people, and I your God." By Jesus, entrance into the "kingdom of God." How may we, from being conceived and born in sin, become children of God? Must be quickened, or made alive, by the breath of God's Spirit, *given to* "*them that ask Him*," who reveals to us how the blood of Christ "can cleanse us

---

* Many may find these lessons too full for a single interview with candidates. They may, of course, be subdivided according to convenience.

PREPARATION LESSONS FOR CANDIDATES. 91

from all sin," 1 Cor. xv. 3. Illustration: From Jewish sacrifices, "My faith would lay her hand," &c. So *Baptismal Prayer*, "Water to the mystical" (or typical) washing away of sin. Jesus Christ, in v. 16, showed Nicodemus the only way of salvation.

II.
WHERE WE STAND AFTER TRUE BAPTISM.

STORY OF PHILIP AND THE EUNUCH. First, and as regards adults, inward baptism, *i.e.*, taking hold of CHRIST'S SUBSTITUTION, Isa. liii. 6. Explain doctrine. Debt paid. Punishment suffered by proxy. Give anecdotes. Show how Christ was counted as the sinner. Outward baptism shows forth death, burial, resurrection, as in chapter above. Old Test. types : (*Opening prayer of Baptismal Service*), Noah, Israel. (Christ circumcised, *baptized*, kept feasts, &c., only "that He might fulfil all righteousness.") Christ's immersion as *our sin-bearer* was under the earth, Rom. vi. 4; Col. ii. 12, iii. 1, &c. *Exhortation after Gospel in Baptismal Service*, with 1 Peter iii. 18, 20, 22. Not the putting away filth of flesh, which is all that water can do, saves us, but the answer of a good conscience towards God by resurrection of Jesus Christ. His resurrection "being quickened by Spirit," the receipt from God for the payment of our debt, for the full bearing of our curse. So, when enabled by the Holy Spirit to take hold of His work for us, we are counted as having died, been buried, and raised up with new lives; freed by death from former guilt, and "have the answer of a good (*i.e.*, perfectly satisfied) conscience" towards God, in whose sight we stand acquitted, "accepted in the Beloved." "He that *believeth*, and is baptized, shall be saved."

III.
PRAYER FOR THE HOLY SPIRIT, AND LIFE.

The reality of prayer. (See 27th Article, "By virtue of prayer unto God," and *4th Prayer and 2nd Exhortation of Baptismal Service*). Illustrations of power of prayer. Great thing asked, "Spiritual regeneration"—that the holy rite may not be an empty form, but may show forth a real passage from death unto life. Prayer no chance experiment. Show certainty of some simple scientific experiment dealing with unseen forces, such as photography; or of unseen natural forces. Astronomers can calculate almanack from certainty of unseen power. "The voice that rolls the stars along spoke all the promises." *The prayer for the Holy Spirit.* Necessity for His work. There may be outward graft on plant, but, without life-principle, it will be dead. So outward joining to the Church, or company of people professing Christ, is accompanied by no real life without the agency of the Lord and Giver of Life. Expectancy of true prayer. Letter put in post, you lose sight of it; but Queen and Government pledged to see to its reaching mark; proved by answers. So we lose sight of prayers, but God is pledged, "Ask, seek, knock, &c."

IV.
THE OATH OF ALLEGIANCE.

1. RENOUNCING. *Illustration: From swearing fealty to earthly monarch.*

1. *Renunciation.* "*Dost thou renounce?*" &c. Meaning of word. Scrip. instances, Abraham, his country; Moses; Pharaoh's court, &c. All that must be left, like old garments stained and soiled, on the other side of the grave: The enemy's livery. WORKS OF DEVIL—specially lies, murder, John viii. 44 (hatred, anger), hindering Gospel (1 Thess. ii. 13), accuser of brethren, Zech. iii., &c. THE WORLD. How can people who have died to the world have their hearts any longer in it? We have been crucified to the world in Christ's person, Gal. vi. 14; are no longer of it, Col. ii. 20. "Why, as though living in it," subject to its fashions and ordinances? What is the world? All such care for and love of things below as interferes with Christ being Lord of our lives and hearts. Not only shown by rich people. Story of Ruth Clark, Mr. Venn's servant. After conversion, accustomed to speak of power the world had exercised over her. "Why, Ruth," said her mistress, "what *world* had you to give up?" "Surely, ma'am, standing at t' yard end with other servants." Ruth found that wasting time in scandal and gossip and foolish talking was her world. Not accept world's standard, *fashion, dress,* pleasures, theatres, balls, &c., *estimates of happiness,* 2 Tim. ii. 4. "*Covetous desires of the same.*" Lot's wife "looking back." "Set your affections on things above; for ye are dead," &c. THE FLESH. Self-indulgence. Illus-

tration from soldier's life, 2 Tim. ii. 3; sloth, impurity of every kind, permission in our presence of loose or doubtful conversation, Col. iii. 5—10; companions, seductive pleasures, doubtful or impure books, railway novels, the first tendencies to self-indulgence in drinking, &c. "Ye have put *off* all these; put *on* therefore," &c. Solemnity of the words, "I RENOUNCE THEM ALL." For life. Some people have thought they could shut out world, flesh, and devil, by going into convents, &c. See what Luther said. How can we overcome? See next Lesson.

V.
OATH OF ALLEGIANCE.

2. BELIEVING. *The victory that overcometh the world.*
"Even our faith." "*Dost thou believe?*" &c. "I BELIEVE." Expand the *Creed*, clause by clause. Difference between head belief and heart belief: we believe in there being an Emperor of China; but does that belief make any difference in our lives? see Rom. x. 9—13, "*With the heart* man believeth unto righteousness." The power to believe is the work of Holy Spirit only. Real belief in Christ is taking him at His word, *trusting* in Him as in a friend, in His blood as in a remedy, in His word as in a promise, and accepting a pardon which He has bought for us. If that acceptance be real, we have passed from death unto life, John v. 24. The old Pomeranian nobles used to stand and say the Creed with drawn swords, to show that they were ready to die for the faith. Are we ready and determined to *live* for it? To die for it if called to do so?

VI.
OATH OF ALLEGIANCE.

3. FULFILLING. "*I will.*"
"*Wilt thou then obediently?*" &c. Binding for ever. One object of our lives to do God's will. Christ did it perfectly. "My meat," &c. "Must be about My Father's business." "Hath not left me alone, for I do always those things which please Him," John viii. 29. "Lo! I come to do Thy will, O God." Resurrection life so ruled and governed by Spirit of God, that we have no desire but to do His will. Like angels, "Do His commandments, hearkening unto voice

of His Word." "Ye are not your own," &c., 1 Cor. vi. 19, 20. "Walk as children of the light." Ten Commandments summed up by Christ in love to God and love to neighbour. Expand, with Sermon on Mount, 1 Cor. xiii., Rom. xii. &c. Will go into all little things of life. Illustrate.

VII.
THE SIGN A SEAL. "*Unto life's end.*"

Water of Baptism the outward and visible sign. Recapitulation from former teaching concerning its deep signification. Necessity that *the inward and spiritual grace* be in the heart. Noble form of words. *Sign of the Cross.* All that it signifies. Christ's cross our one hope. We are crucified to the world. We follow Him, "bearing His cross." Illustrate from old Crusaders, "*Soldier, servant,*" "not ashamed." Expand the double profession, "Ashamed of Jesus! shall it be?" &c. Anecdotes of faithfulness unto death (Madagascar Martyrs, &c.). "*Unto his life's end.*" In marriage, closest earthly union, vows are exchanged, "*till death us do part.*" In Baptism, showing forth closest spiritual union, marriage of soul to Christ (Rom. vii. 4) *till death us do unite.* Let the words ring always in our ears—in temptation, sorrow, sickness, death, "Be thou faithful unto death, and I will give thee a crown of life." "*Under Christ's banner.*" "His banner over me was *love.*" "Fighting manfully." Illustration from military anecdotes. What an honour to be allowed to make open confession! If it means anything, means for life, death, eternity. "Oft in sorrow, oft in woe, onward, Christians, onward go!" Meaning of a "*Christian* name," Acts xi. 26. Our names reminders of our vows. Baptism an outward seal of God's covenant promises to usward who believe.

VIII.
THE CHARGE TO THE BAPTIZED.

Where do we stand? "Regenerated," inwardly regenerated, or born again, if we have really been baptized by Holy Spirit, and become true Christians: washed, sanctified, justified, 1 Cor. vi. 11; "Born of water and spirit," *i.e.*, washed in Christ's blood, quickened by His Spirit. In any case *outwardly* joined and professedly made members of the company of Christians called Christ's Church.

Thanksgiving in Baptismal Service. For what? For our being translated into kingdom of Jesus Christ, out of kingdom of Satan, and for having been made heirs of eternal life. Full meaning of this glorious condition. Illustration from Scripture references. In adult Baptism, no person has a right to admission unless he have repented and believed, Acts ix. 37; and this believing translates him unto Christ's kingdom. Art. xxxvii., "They which receive baptism rightly." *Parting charge in Baptismal Service.* "Walk answerably to your Christian calling." "As children of the light." Let "I have been baptized" answer temptations to wrong, to carelessness. Need of holiness. Christ not only "Sacrifice for sin," also "Ensample of godly life." "I am the Lord's," your motto; "Holiness unto the Lord," written on all you say and do. Old motto, "*Noblesse oblige!*" Put the thought into other words, "Walk as becometh saints." "I am a Christian." "What manner of persons ought ye to be?" Expand on the position of pardon, perfect acceptance in the Son; covered over in Him. "Hast loved them as thou hast loved Me?" Christ has "received us to the glory of God." "If children, then heirs." "All things are yours, for ye are Christ's, and Christ is God's."

> "I have taken a last farewell
> Of a life of sin and shame;
> My heart with the King must dwell,
> Who am called by a Christian name.
> My armour must all be bright,
> For here in a foeman's land
> In the battle I daily fight
> For the Lord, in whose ranks I stand
>
> "Till the Master himself shall come,
> His will I would here obey;
> Till His messenger calls me home,
> I must seek to prepare His way;
> Till my sight shall in death grow dim,
> I would daily His love adore;
> *I have given my life to Him,*
> *He will keep it for evermore.*"

CHAPTER VII.

ON PREPARATION FOR CONFIRMATION.

"And now I should like to know your reason for wishing to be confirmed?"

"Please, sir, to take my sins upon myself."

"And what difference will your Confirmation make in your life?"

"Please, ma'am, never have no more pleasures as long as I live."

Such have been the questions, and such the answers, attending applications for admission to a Confirmation-class on the part of thoroughly well-meaning candidates. And it is with the conviction that such ignorance is far more general than is commonly supposed, and in the hope that plans found to work usefully in one district may be attended with benefit in others, that the following hints are offered for the consideration of Bible-class teachers upon whom may devolve the task of preparation for this important ordinance of our Church.

In the arrangement of Teacher' Confirmation-classes there will, of course, be due consultation with the clergyman to whose parish they belong; and times and occasions of instruction will by him be so ordered as best to supplement the general and individual teaching which he may be able to give. In large town parishes, or in scattered country districts—and such are very particularly in the mind of the writer—the incumbent will frequently be anxious that the sub-classes (if we may use such a term) of the Bible-class teachers shall include candidates not ordinarily numbered among their hearers, whose circumstances, local or otherwise, may render it specially desirable that they should receive the minute individual teaching which few clergymen thus circumstanced are able to give. Often a Confirmation season will thus furnish an important accession of numbers to the Bible-class; candidates, at first but temporarily united to the teacher, being ranked after the Confirmation among its regular members.

The teacher's Confirmation-class will, probably, be held once or twice a week; while individual interviews with candidates, such as have been already more generally considered, will form a very leading feature in the course of preparation. Two or three such interviews seem to us the least with which the thorough-going teacher can satisfy himself. The first will, of course, be on occasion of the candidate's giving in his name as such; and to this visit will especially belong the private inquiry into his reason for so doing, and the establishment—if such has not previously existed—of a settled confidence between teacher and hearer, deepened by the solemnity of the subject at this time bringing them together.

The teacher will do well to cement union of spirit among the Confirmation candidates, leading them, as far as possible, to regard their association in the classes, and in the approaching service of dedication, as very real and binding. When it can be done without much difficulty, it will be found a good plan to arrange for a country walk, in which, perhaps more than once, the members of the Confirmation-class may have an opportunity of unfettered intercourse with each other; the teacher taking advantage of the occasion, not only for gaining an insight into individual tastes and characters, but also for an interchange of thought and conversation with members of the class hitherto looking somewhat shyly upon a more formal interview. On these, as on all other occasions, he will himself find the importance of utilising such intercourse for the establishment of real friendship with members of his class—of a friendship often outlasting changes of place and time, and of which it may be that eternity alone will reveal the depth and sacredness.

But it is time that, leaving the outer machinery of the Confirmation-class, we turn to the subject itself, and to the question as to the course along which Confirmation preparation may be best guided. And at this point we would venture to refer the reader to the chapter on Adult Baptism immediately preceding our present one, and to suggest that, when the Confirmation-class is found to include many who have never had the opportunity of receiving thorough religious teaching, much of the instruction then proposed should form the basis of that laid out for the candidates.

Our lost condition by nature, the necessity for atonement, Christ's Substitution, the need of His Holy Spirit enabling us to take hold of that Substitution, and the position in which we stand when thus joined to, or "baptized into, Christ," are distinct topics, already enlarged upon as much at length as time and space will admit. Even in the case of well-instructed candidates, it will be desirable to dwell once more on the first stages of all religious instruction as laid down for us in the Word of God, and which may be briefly comprehended in the showing forth of the two positions, to one or other of which each must of necessity belong—that of the sinner in the world without Christ, and that of the sinner saved by and united to Christ.

Oh! that to all of us who are teachers it might be given so to dwell on these fundamental truths, so to press upon the hearers, in too many instances applying for Confirmation as a mere formality belonging to their "being grown-up," the necessity for fleeing to a crucified Saviour—for seeking in Him a refuge from the windy storm and tempest,—that, even before the setting forth of teaching distinctively belonging to the rite itself, there might be a stirring and awakening of soul, a sounding of depths in spirit and conscience hitherto unruffled by any deeper conviction than a general sense of the necessity of "being good," and a cry from the ground of the heart, "What shall I do to be saved?"

In this primary instruction—instruction here summed up in few words, but really containing the very essence of "life and death teaching"—the teacher will spare no pains, no thought, no previous preparation. He will, in some cases, have much to sweep away. He will have to solemnize those who have thought lightly of Confirmation, by their seeing in him one who regards the matter as for eternity. He will have to bring home to them that not the outward ordinance however important, and however much to be held in reverent esteem, but the soul-dedication which it represents, is the engrossing matter for their consideration. He will have to make use of a short time of opportunity, during which parents and masters are willing to make concessions for candidates' attendance, with the reflection that such an opportunity may not occur again, and that to the Great Teacher who has honoured him by placing the work in his hand he must give account concerning the souls thus, for a space at least, committed to his guidance.

It will probably be at the third or fourth meeting of the Confirmation-class that the line of instruction will diverge from that already suggested as suitable for candidates for Adult Baptism. Confirmation candidates will be reminded that they were in their infancy promised to Christ; that their names were set down to be on the Lord's side; that "repentance and faith" (and how much is comprised in these two words they will have already been taught) were, even as explained in the Catechism, the conditions upon which the title of "Christian" was conferred upon them; and the question will arise as to whether those conditions have as yet been fulfilled, or, in other words, as to whether they have as yet passed from death unto life.

It would be superfluous here to enter at any length into the grounds on which we of the Church of England regard Infant Baptism to be right and scriptural, but it will be the duty of the teacher to stir up to thought and serious inquiry those who may never have troubled themselves to reflect upon the subject.

1. A primary ground for the admission of infants by Baptism into the outward Church of Christ is the analogy between Baptism and Circumcision, whereby at eight days old the Jewish infant was admitted into the Jewish Church, and into outward covenant with God. Abraham believed and was circumcised, and after him his posterity, at this earliest stage of infancy, were circumcised; and the early Christians believed and were baptized, and after them their children were, as infants, consecrated to the Lord in Baptism. In both cases the reality at first preceded the sign; and in both cases the sign afterwards preceded the reality which it was to show forth. The very absence of any prohibition of Infant Baptism would in itself be an argument for its adoption—the Christ of the New Testament, who said, "Suffer little children to come unto Me, and forbid them not," being assuredly as willing that the children of the New dispensation should be dedicated to Him as that those of the Old should be. In His parting charge—"Go ye into all the world and preach the Gospel to every creature, baptizing them in the name of the Father, and of the Son, and of the Holy Ghost" —there was no exclusive clause forbidding the little ones to be brought to Him; and thus to parents, at the very outset of their children's lives, Baptism seems to stand as a reminder that those children have been given them for the service of God, and that they must

see to it that on their part it be no unmeaning ceremony. It will be well, further, to notice the analogy between the Jewish and the Christian rites traced out by St. Paul in the second and third chapters of the Colossians.

2. In the notice of Apostolic Baptisms in Acts xvi. 15, xvi. 33, and 1 Cor. i. 16, we read that whole households were baptized after the conversion of their heads; and it is more than unlikely that children should have been absent from each of these collected families.

3. Further, Justin Martyr, Irenæus, Tertullian, Origen, and other ancient historic writers, testify to the fact of Infant Baptism having been handed down in the Church from Apostolic ages.

Thus much laid down, the question will follow as to the position occupied by the baptized candidate for Confirmation.

"I wish you to see where you stand," the teacher will say, after bringing before his hearers the scene of their own Baptism as infants, and its noble words of consecration; "I do not want you to think that your Baptism, when you were too young to understand it, meant nothing. If it meant anything at all, if your parents and your godparents were not trifling before Him to whom they gave you, it meant that you were sworn in for the Lord's service; that they promised for you that you should, when old enough, regard yourselves as having been pledged to become in this world, where all men are divided into the armies of Christ and the armies of His enemies, His faithful soldiers unto your lives' end.

"It may be," he will be led to add, "that some among you will say, 'Why am I to be bound by engagements which were made for me without my having the power to resist them? These things were promised and vowed in my name without the possibility of consent, or the reverse, on my part, and therefore I do not see why I should be held responsible for their being kept.'"

And here the teacher may, with all the pictorial power at his command, represent the case of some infant heir to an estate held from a feudal sovereign in olden times on certain conditions, such as, for instance, that of bringing a certain number of retainers into the field in case of war or needed service. On the event of the father's death during the child's infancy, would not its guardian promise in the infant's name the fulfilment of such conditions, until he should be of age to inquire into and fulfil them himself? And, even before the solemn ratification of the oaths of tenure, they would instil into his mind the duties of his position, and of loyalty to his liege lord; and thus the boy might be led in heart and in soul to reverence and follow him, only longing for the outward and formal declaration of his vows of service.

"And so," the teacher will continue, "you had promised for you the fulfilment of conditions upon which your name was entered on the roll of those who are called Christians—of those accounted, on their fulfilment, children of God, members of Christ, and inheritors of the kingdom of heaven. You would not have wished your parents and friends to have neglected thus to have stood as sureties for you. If they were in earnest they then did you good service, and they have since brought you up to know the Lord, to see the necessity of that death unto sin, and that faith or belief in a crucified Saviour, which constitute the true spiritual Baptism prefigured by that of water to which they brought you. In any case, it is for you to determine *now* whether you will yourselves stand forth to say publicly that you are on the Lord's side."

And here, while dwelling on the loving disposition of the Head of the Church towards those brought to Him in Baptism, the teacher will feel it his duty to show that those outwardly baptized, who care not to seek for themselves the real Baptism of heart and soul which marks the transition from death unto life, share their condemnation who in olden time, having been circumcised with the circumcision made with hands, had desired nothing of that death to the world and life unto God which the Jewish rite also showed forth. "He is not a Jew which is one outwardly, neither is that circumcision which is outward in the flesh: but he is a Jew which is one inwardly; and circumcision is that of the heart, in the Spirit, and not in the letter, whose praise is not of men but of God."

And even so, when there has been the resistance of the strivings of God's Spirit in the hearts of those brought to outward Baptism, it must be remembered that such a denial of all that Christ's Sacrament was intended to convey increases their condemnation before Him. He that *believeth* and is baptized shall be saved. The praying parents and god-parents of infants brought to Baptism have a right to plead their having so dedicated the child as entitling them to expect God's fulfilment of the promises. He who ordained Baptism and commanded it for His Church, will never disown His own Ordinance, and the child (and we would remind children often of their Baptism) passing from infancy to boyhood or girlhood, and realising the struggle against sin in an evil world, and feeling its own weakness and the greatness of the enemies which it must face, has a right to plead with Him to whom it was early dedicated the promises which belonged to that dedication, and to claim a greater and larger gift of the Spirit of God than that measure of His holy teaching which has already lit up some of the recesses of its soul, and shown it the need of a Saviour. He who is more ready to hear than we to pray, will never forget His promises where He stands as a covenant God. "He will ever be mindful of His covenant."

Having thus endeavoured to show forth to his hearers their position as baptized members at all events of the outward and visible Church of Christ, the teacher will have cleared the way to the next point on which he will have to enlarge—that, namely, set forth in the preface to the Confirmation Service. It will be for him to remind them of the reasonableness of an institution which calls upon children "arrived at years of discretion," to inquire into the undertaking made for them by sureties at their Baptism, and to come forward and publicly to take their stand on the Lord's side. He will have to dwell, in passing, on the words, "*the Church* hath thought good to order," in order to mark that the rite of Confirmation, though sacred, reasonable, and fitting, as a complement to Infant Baptism, is not of Divine command; and will have to guard against any confusion in the minds of candidates who might associate it with the laying on of hands permitted for the imparting of extraordinary and miraculous gifts, mentioned in Apostolic ages. In all Protestant churches an adult confession of Christianity is required by those baptized as infants; though in some, as, for instance, in the Scotch Church, such a confession is regarded as implied and made on the occasion of First Communion.

In the "*hereafter*" of our Church of England

Preface he will also trace a marked intimation of the *Reformed* character of our present Confirmation ritual, Confirmation having, previously to the days of our Protestant Reformers, been regarded as a sort of appendage immediately following Infant Baptism, whereby, from the laying on of episcopal hands, some special and mysterious grace was conferred on the unconscious child.

And again, candidates will be called to observe that the word "*Confirmation*" does not only imply that the bishop, by invoking God's blessing upon them, and uniting in prayer for them with the assembled congregation, confirms, by strengthening and establishing them in their resolution henceforth to serve the Lord; but, further, that they themselves are called upon actively to confirm and ratify before God and the congregation those vows which were made for them at their Baptism.

And at this point the teacher will endeavour to set forth before his hearers the solemnity of the question publicly asked, and publicly answered,—the full meaning of that "I DO" which is for life, even as is the "I WILL" of Adult Baptism; and will use all earnestness and entreaty with those for whose instruction he is responsible, that they may fully weigh the extent of its meaning,

Of course he will here, enlarging from the summaries

in the Church Catechism, enter into the full meaning of that Baptismal Vow to which it refers; he will show from Scripture its depth, fulness, and responsibilities, and will remind those before him that it would indeed be a vain thing for them thus to take up their banners, could they not rest their hearts, and assure themselves of strength, in the first utterance of their newly consecrated life, "Our help is in the name of the Lord." (Comp. Exod. xxxiv. 5—7.)

It will be needless here to dwell further on the simple and beautiful Confirmation Service; on the earnest prayers, on the paternal reception of the young confessors among the servants of Christ; on the "Thine for ever" of the benedictory prayer; on the supplication that the Fatherly hand may be ever over them, the Holy Spirit ever near to guide them, and that theirs may in the end be everlasting life. We refer those readers who may care to enlarge more fully upon the service of life-long dedication to Christ, to the notes drawn out on Adult Baptism, appended to the previous chapter.

It remains for us to suggest one or two plans for rendering the Confirmation-day one of solemn and lasting impression to those taking part in it.

The last meeting of the candidates will be one of very serious and earnest review of the previous instruction; and the private interview, which will furnish the final opportunity of personal appeal and pleading with the individual members of the class, will convey to each one the assurance of the teacher's individual remembrance and sympathy. This will be particularly needed in many cases where, from the nature of the home surroundings to which too many candidates return, there will be danger lest reverence be blunted, and the solemn occasion be regarded lightly.

One difficulty peculiar to the preparation of female candidates is the tendency to regard the Confirmation-day as an occasion for a display of dress only too well calculated to take off the attention of the wearers from the service itself. A teacher with strong personal influence will often be able to counteract this by a simple entreaty addressed to members of the class, that they will not grieve her by leading her to anxiety on this account; and, where the candidates are from a very poor class, she will often be able herself to supply the neat cap and modest cape, which they might be unable to provide, and which will give them a quiet and uniform appearance.

All previous arrangements for ensuring punctuality at the church, and for the prevention of the least hurry and confusion on the Confirmation-day, are now, happily, so much regarded as to make it superfluous here to dwell upon them. In the country, and, indeed, often in towns, where the distance from the church is considerable, such arrangements, and those for refreshment and rest after the service, may involve some trouble on the part of the clergymen's families, and, possibly, of the teachers'; but it need hardly be said how well bestowed will be every effort to prevent flurry and confusion on a day which should be one through life associated with loving welcome, recognised brotherhood, and individual sympathy.

When feasible, an evening meeting of the candidates, and of all the other members of the Bible-class able to attend, will be found a plan attended with very useful results. This meeting of welcome, in a class well known to the writer, has been made the occasion of giving to each one a memorial card, glazed or ornamented, such as is shown (though necessarily in plain style and contracted form) on the following page—the hymn having been already sung in the church; and a Confirmation motto is always written, with full Christian name, on the back. A ribbon is passed through the top of the card, by which it may be hung up as a memento of the day. These cards have been found, years after Confirmation, carefully treasured, and often referred to by those who then received them.

This hymn, and the favourite "*O happy day, that fixed my choice,*" to its own sweet tune, have generally begun and concluded the short address of greeting belonging to this gathering. It has generally been the teacher's aim to associate with it a text of warning,

"𝕿hine for ever."

Confirmation.

"Choose ye this day whom ye will serve."
"Thou art my portion, O Lord; I have said that I would keep Thy words."
"Hold Thou me up, and I shall be safe."
"My grace is sufficient for Thee."

O Lord, Thy heavenly grace impart,
And fix my frail, inconstant heart:
Henceforth my chief desire shall be
To dedicate myself to Thee:
        To Thee, my God, to Thee!

Thy glorious eye pervadeth space;
Thou'rt present, Lord, in every place;
And wheresoe'er my lot may be,
Still shall my spirit cleave to Thee:
        To Thee, my God, to Thee!

Whate'er pursuits my time employ,
One thought shall fill my soul with joy:
That silent, secret thought shall be
That all my hopes are fixed on Thee:
        On Thee, my God, on Thee!

Renouncing every worldly thing.
Safe 'neath the shadow of Thy wing.
My sweetest thought henceforth shall be,
That all I want I find in Thee:
        In Thee, my God, in Thee!

The love of Christ constraineth us, because we thus judge, that if one died for all, then were all dead; and that He died for all, that they which live should not henceforth live unto themselves, but unto Him which died for them, and rose again.

St. M——'s Church, B——.
——— 187 .

"𝕿hou art 𝔐ine."

and another of promise, upon which a few earnest words have been spoken, and which have also been previously written at the back of the card in readiness for presentation. Such a combination have been Ps. lxxviii. 9, and Rev. ii. 10, "*Be thou faithful unto death, and I will give thee a crown of life;*" Ps. xx. 5, "*In the name of our God will we set up our banners,*" with 2 Tim. ii. 4, and Sol. Song ii. 4, "*His banner over me was love.*" Some more substantial gift in the form of a book may sometimes, in the case of teachers able to afford it, form a suitable Confirmation gift.

In closing this chapter, the writer must admit to having touched only on the leading points of preparation for Confirmation. Too much stress cannot be laid on the importance of this opportunity for sowing a harvest which may be reaped hereafter in its fulness; and whether these chapters be read in some distant hamlet, far removed from the immediate supervision of the mother-church, or whether in some town district, where the greatness of the population leaves to the clergyman's fellow-workers more of the responsibility of preparation for this sacred and solemn ordinance than would otherwise fall to their share, none, surely, will, as teachers, enter upon or continue their work without the constant prayer that it may be with them as with the prophet of old, concerning whom it is written, "*The Lord was with him, and did let none of his words fall to the ground.*"

CHAPTER VIII.

ON PREPARATION FOR THE LORD'S SUPPER.

"*Wherefore take this holy Sacrament to your comfort.*" It is surely one clearly-marked duty of the Bible-class teacher frequently to echo in the ears of his hearers this invitation, sent to believers by the Lord Himself; and, in view of the small numbers of communicants furnished from adult classes, compared with those of their confirmed members, we are sometimes inclined to ask whether it has with sufficient solemnity been placed before all sharing the weekly instruction, that the commandment of Christ to " do this in remembrance" is as clear, as binding, and as perpetual as that concerning Baptism, or as any other which He delivered to His Church; that those who are not in a condition to come to His table are certainly not ready to meet death; that, in short, it is quite time that we who are teachers should bestir ourselves to consider whether we are urging this duty with sufficient solemnity upon those under our guidance. May it not be that some are remaining away through timidity, who would most assuredly meet the Master's welcome at His sacred ordinance? while there may be others to whom the testing question, "Why do not you come to the Communion?" might bring home a conviction that reasons preventing their obedience to this their Lord's command are, perhaps, the same which are keeping them away from coming to Him altogether.

The conscientious teacher will spare no effort to secure to the members of his Bible-class a thorough knowledge of the meaning and history of the Lord's Supper, and will earnestly endeavour to prevent anything like a trifling and ignorant approach to so sacred a privilege. It will often be difficult to carry out this view of his duty. A Confirmation-day has many externals marking it as an occasion of especial note. There is a bishop; and there are white dresses; and people come to it from all parts; and "it's right for young people that they should attend to such a time— I did myself when I was young;" and the teacher gains his point: and so the attendance of the candidate at the Confirmation-class and at the church is conceded by masters and employers. But the Christ-ordained observance recurring periodically in every church— that ordinance to which belongs no outward display, which takes up time at regular intervals, but on which regular attendance is an exception—is often looked upon with comparatively little interest, often, indeed, as a mere occasion for "some folks setting themselves above others;" and the teacher will have very frequently to receive members of his Sacramental-class in twos and threes (as can best be arranged), if he is to secure for them any special or consecutive instruction on so deeply important a matter.

"I thought it was only for gentry folk;" "I went once after we was confirmed when I was a girl; we all did, to oblige the clergyman!" "I don't see that I ain't as good as many as does go, and thinks a deal of theirselves." These were three consecutive answers received by the writer from parents or employers of Bible-class candidates on whom the seriousness of the matter had been pressed; and this, not in a low East London neighbourhood, unpenetrated even by the sound of the Gospel, but in a "highly respectable district," from which church and chapel goers were numerous, but a district, nevertheless, in which the idea was, some time ago, by no means uncommon that "now the Registration Act had come in, Baptism had pretty much gone out."

And it is this intense and heathenish carelessness on the one side, and an equally ignorant superstition on the other, attaching to the Sacrament of the Lord's Supper the idea of a mystic rite to which few dare approach, that, in the minds of many of his hearers, will have to be counteracted by the teacher's earnest effort to convey to them the simple Gospel teaching concerning its sacred obligations.

It need hardly be remarked that his example as a regular and earnest Communicant, and his constant influence, will be to set before them as a great and highly-to-be-prized privilege that of admission to the Lord's Table; and there are probably few Bible-class teachers who have for any length of time prayed and laboured for those to whom they stand in so near a relationship, who will not testify to the close tie which unites together the little band year after year privileged to draw nigh with faith, and together to "take this holy Sacrament to their comfort."

The first lesson in the course of Sacramental preparation should always be on *the Passover*. The description of the night on which the Paschal lamb was first slain cannot be too solemnly, too circumstantially, pictured to the hearers; and the various chief Passovers linking it to the Paschal feasts of our Lord's time may be touched upon, so as to prevent there being a total absence of connection in the minds of the learners between the Passover in Egypt and those of the New Testament.

The Paschal lamb, and the ritual belonging to the institution of that "night to be much remembered," will thus be in the thoughts of his class when, on occasion of the next lesson, the teacher dwells on the night to be yet more remembered—the night of the last Supper and of the Upper Chamber, the night in which He who was the true Paschal Lamb partook of that sacrifice wherein He alone, who knew no sin, had no atonement, keeping the observance which for 1,500 years had shone through the twilight of the world's history as a watch-fire kept on from generation to generation, until the true Light should Himself shine.

The teacher will bid his hearers mark with him how, point by point, the old Jewish festival on this evening lost itself in the Christ-ordained memorial Feast. He will remind them that many additional observances had gathered round the Paschal celebration since its institution, some of which, at all events, our Lord (who, as man, regarded the customs and ordinances of the Jews) undoubtedly followed, as He presided at the board; and will point out how the Divine Saviour adapted the non-sacrificial elements of the Feast—the bread and the wine—to be the emblematic memorials of His great love when He should have given His flesh for the life of the world.

The order of participation will be most clearly seen by a comparison of the chief points of the ceremonial as given by the Jewish Rabbis, with the New Testament narrative:—

ON PREPARATION FOR THE LORD'S SUPPER. 119

Ceremonial of the Passover according to Jewish records.

Notices of Christ's celebration of the Feast as contained in the New Testament.

The first ceremony was, "*The blessing of the wine.*" The master of the feast *gave thanks* over a cup of wine as follows:—"Blessed be Thou, O Lord our God, King of the universe, who hast created the *fruit of the vine!*" Then, for the day:—"Blessed be Thou for this good day, and for this holy convocation which Thou hast given us for joy and rejoicing. Blessed be Thou, O Lord, who hast sanctified Israel and the times." Then the wine was partaken of by all present.

Luke xxii. 17.—"And He took *the cup* and *gave thanks*, and said, Take this and divide it among yourselves. For I say unto you, I will not drink of the *fruit of the vine* until the kingdom of God shall come."

The hands were then washed, and the table furnished with the Paschal lamb, bitter herbs, two cakes of unleavened bread, remains of peace offerings of the preceding day, and the charosheth or thick sauce, into which each person dipped the bitter herbs before partaking of them.

After some further ceremonial observances of little importance, the dishes being for a season removed, the children, or if there were none, the last of the guests, inquired, "What mean ye by this service?" Then followed the "*showing forth.*" The master of the feast replied in a liturgical form, "How different is this night from all other nights, &c. This passover which we eat is in respect that the Lord passed over the houses of our fathers in Egypt!" Then followed more detailed explanations concerning the Paschal lamb, unleavened

It is probable that St. Paul alludes to this custom of the Paschal feast in the words, "As often as ye eat this bread and drink this cup, bread, and bitter herbs, concluding with the ascription of praise:—"Therefore are we bound to confess, to praise, to laud, to glorify, to honour, to extol, to magnify, and to ascribe victory to Him who did unto our fathers and to us all these signs, and who brought us forth from servitude to freedom, from sorrow to joy, from darkness to marvellous light, and we say before Him halleluiah!"

ye do *show* the Lord's death till He come."—1 Cor. xi. 26.

The 113th and 114th Psalms were then repeated, with blessings and prayer. The second cup of wine was partaken of, and after fresh washing of hands, the participation of the feast began.

The master of the feast, taking one of the cakes of unleavened bread, broke it, and after blessing it and giving thanks, divided a piece to each person separately, all devoutly eating it.

Matt. xxvi. 26; Luke xxii. 19; 1 Cor. xi. 24. "And as they were eating," "He took bread, and gave thanks, and brake it, and said, Take, eat: this is My body which is broken for you; this do in remembrance of Me."

The rest of the cake, with bitter herbs, was then eaten, each person dipping into the charosheth or sauce.

Matt. xxvi. 21.—"And as they did eat, He said, Verily I say unto you, that one of you shall betray Me. And they were exceeding sorrowful, and began every one of them to say unto Him, Lord, is it I? And He answered and said, He that dippeth his hand with Me in the dish, the same shall betray Me. . . . Then Judas which betrayed Him answered and said, Master, is it I? He said unto him, Thou hast said."

Then, after a participation in the peace-offerings, the PASCHAL LAMB was eaten; discourse being carried on in appropriate manner, and in accordance with the occupation.

Here followed the "*Cup of Blessing,*" or benediction, which the master of the feast handed round to each person, offering therewith thanksgiving for the deliverance from Egypt, for the covenant of circumcision, and for the Law of Moses.

1 Cor. xi. 25; Matt. xxvi. 28.—"After the same manner also He took the cup when He had supped, saying, This cup is the New Testament (covenant) in My blood: this do ye as oft as ye drink it *in remembrance of Me.*" Or, according to St. Matthew:—"For this is My blood of the new covenant, which is shed for many for the remission of sins. But I say unto you, I will not drink henceforth of this fruit of the vine until that day when I drink it new with you in My Father's kingdom."

1 Cor. x. 16.—"The *cup of blessing* which we bless, is it not the communion of the blood of Christ?"

The feast concluded with the singing of the closing psalms of the great "*Halleluiah,*" or hymn of praise, being from the 113th to the 118th Psalm inclusive.

Matt. xxvi. 30.—"And when they had sung an hymn (*mary.*—psalm) they went out into the Mount of Olives."

And here the teacher will dwell, point by point, on this strange and solemn ceremonial of the Paschal night.

That first cup delivered to the disciples with so new a form of words, the "fruit of the vine," which they were to divide among themselves, why was it thus presented? What meant that sudden flash of anticipation, that glimpse of the marriage-supper *of the Lamb*, which would take place when the kingdom of God should come, wherein those for whom He was about to drain the bitter cup of agony should be presented spotless before Him, the fruit of the travail of His soul? Was it that the glad ascription of praise seemed too jubilant a song for the Man of Sorrows, as the hour and the power of darkness drew on, that He now refused the cup of thanksgiving? Was it the thought that, although He was about to pour out His soul unto death to bring in "a good day" "for joy and rejoicing" to a sanctified Israel, yet to the greater number of those for whom His blood would be shed His cry would still be, "Is it nothing to you, all ye that pass by? behold and see if there be any sorrow like unto My sorrow wherewith the Lord hath afflicted Me in the day of His fierce anger. This I have borne for you, and yet ye will not come unto Me that ye may have life?"

What a wondrous "*showing forth*" must that have been which followed! How must each disciple have felt assured, as he listened to the oft-told story of the deliverance from Egypt which came from the Master's lips, that, though as yet they fully understood it not, there dwelt in His speech a reference to a bondage darker than Egypt's, to a deliverance more costly, more triumphant. Never, surely, had Paschal feast such a shower-forth. Never with so deep a signification did the ascription of praise resound for the translation "from servitude to freedom, from sorrow to joy, and from darkness to marvellous light."

And as the sun set over the hills of Jerusalem,* there faded with it the last day of that Jewish dispensation wherein the types and shadows of the law should faintly figure forth the mighty Sacrifice, which, in the new day now probably beginning, would be accomplished. For the last time would the Paschal lamb be slain in order to the showing forth of a future Redeemer. For the last time would the going forth from Egypt be remembered as the symbol of a deliverance yet to come from a darker than Egyptian bondage. For now, as in a dissolving view, the shadow was fading into the brighter reality; the dim types of the Passover were about to be swallowed up in their great fulfilment. The sun went down upon a dispensation of rites and ceremonies. When he should next sink to his rest, it would be over a world redeemed, yet brought out into the Gospel dispensation by so tremendous a sacrifice that his own rays would be veiled in a cloud of thick darkness, as though that wondrous transaction between the Father and the Son

---

* It must be remembered that the Jewish days were always calculated from sunset to sunset.

were too solemn and too mysterious to be witnessed by the rude light of day.

Solemnly was that commencing day ushered in by Him who, ere its close, would, in His sacred person, have borne the sin of many, and yielded up His life as the atonement for the whole world. Taking in His hand the unleavened cake always divided at this period of the feast, He brake it, and distributed it to each one with a new meaning and a new form of words :— "*Take, eat, this is my body which is broken for you. This do in remembrance of Me.*"

Neither the sorrowful questionings concerning the announcement which followed of the one betrayer who yet sat at the table of the Lord, nor the solemn participation in the flesh of the Paschal lamb, can have dismissed from the disciples' thoughts that mournful admonition. What could it signify ? The broken bread speaking of a body broken for them—this lowly remembrance of humiliation—did this betoken the glorious setting up of an earthly kingdom, in which they, as faithful followers, should share His exaltation ? It yet remained for them to hear and understand the words spoken by their Master on that awful night, " My kingdom is not of this world."

And when the Feast was ended, and there only remained the participation in the final " cup of blessing," and as they awaited the thanksgiving with which it was wontedly accompanied, for the deliverance from Egypt, and for the covenant of circumcision, and for the law of Moses, there was once more introduced a change in the liturgy of the Passover service. In giving them the wine, which was evermore to be taken in remembrance of Him, Christ spoke of a greater deliverance—a deliverance from the bondage of sin, and from the legal bondage of the law by "*remission* of sins," and of a new covenant which left no place for the old, and of a kingdom in the glory of the Father, of which the blood-shedding, betokened by that fruit of the vine, was the charter and the pledge; and He bade them drink all of this "in remembrance of Me;" "for it is shed for you, and for many, for the remission of sins."

How simple, yet how wondrous, those words! How far-stretching beyond the end of time into eternity! Christ was to be offered *once for all*. No more telling period of the repast could have been selected for the appointment of the memorial type than that wherein the old covenant was remembered which should be lost in the new, and the law given by Moses, which should for ever show forth in glorious contrast the grace and truth which came by Jesus Christ.

When the cup of blessing had passed round which brought those sorrowful disciples so near to each other and to their Lord, the Jewish sacrificial Passover was over; the Christian memorial feast, whose sweetest, simplest name is "the Lord's Supper," had been instituted. It was time that the hymn should be sung with which closed the Paschal festival.

Then, probably, ascended from the upper chamber the Psalms of the Paschal Liturgy; lofty strains, which He alone of that little band, who afterwards opened their understanding, that they should understand all that was written in the Psalms concerning Himself, could comprehend in their fulness of prophetic meaning.

In the bugle-call of the 117th Psalm, summoning all nations to praise the LORD, He would discern the hidden note of prophecy afterwards taken up and re-echoed by His Apostle,* whereby, at first softly, then more loudly, it was proclaimed to the world that Gentile peoples of all tribes and kindreds should have *their* part in that song of praise, and should show forth the merciful kindness and truth which met together in the gift of the Son of God, sent forth for the salvation of "all people." And if here the strain became more jubilant, and the prophetic 118th Psalm resounded which in interchanging parts showed forth the triumph and exaltation of the Messiah of whom it testified, must not that suffering Messiah have wondered—if wonder to Him were possible—that by Him alone

* Rom. xv. 8, 9, 11.

was understood all that is foretold concerning Himself? Had those who with Him united in the solemn service realised their mighty import, with what a fulness of adoration would they have taken up the strain that from century to century had meetly closed that Halleluiah Chorus of the Paschal feast—"*O give thanks unto the* LORD, *for* HE *is good ; for* HIS *mercy endureth for ever !*"

We have thus dwelt on the circumstances attending the institution of the Lord's Supper from a strong conviction that if the teacher would bring home to his hearers the position which it occupies, and the love which ordained it, he must, in pictorial fashion, show forth the transition from the ancient Paschal Feast to the Christ-ordained Memorial Festival.

We now proceed to the next part of the preparation for Communion with which, to our thinking, the teacher will engage his class, *i.e., the exact significance of this Sacrament.**

---

* This word is not a Scriptural one, but was by the Romans used to designate the sacred military oath of allegiance to the Emperor. Afterwards, the early Christians adopted the word sacrament as generally meaning *sacred thing*, to which simple signification there was further added the idea of something allegorical. Thus, the brazen serpent, typifying Christ, was called a "sacrament." The idea of symbolism came at last to be always attached to the word, which, later on, was exclusively applied to sacred religious ordinances. As superstition increased, there was associated with the word sacrament the under-

And, firstly, like the Passover, it is *a Memorial Feast*. ,' This do *in remembrance* of Me." How simple was our Lord's command! He took the ordinary articles of food,—bread and wine,—and delivered them to each of His disciples, bidding them thus show forth amongst themselves that breaking of His Body and outpouring of His Blood whereby He should redeem them.

When any dearly loved friends or relatives have been removed from us, how eagerly do we treasure up every remembrance of them! Each look and word is, as far as possible, recalled. Every recollection of their habits of thought and speech, of the walks we shared with them, of the rooms wherein they dwelt, of the occupations wherein they were wont to engage, is held sacred.

But how much more should each remembrance rest

standing of a mysterious inward grace attendant upon outward signs, when ministered by an ordained priest, and to be communicated irrespectively of the receiver's faith. Thus, the Roman Catholic Church asserts that there are seven Sacraments :—Baptism, Confirmation, Holy Orders, Penance, Marriage, the Eucharist, and Extreme Unction. Our reformed Church of England, when it put aside doctrines and commandments of men, and determined to take Scripture for its only guide, rejected these false views. It retained the word *sacrament*, with the early meaning of an outward sign of an inward and spiritual grace; but declared that it must have been "ordained as such by Christ Himself;" thus limiting the Sacraments to Baptism and the Lord's Supper. And our Reformers further maintained that the benefit of the Sacrament lay not in the external, priestly administration, but in the right, believing, spiritual reception thereof by the person to whom it was administered.

in our hearts of Him who gave His life for His friends! Each remembrance of His dying hours, each word that fell from His lips during the night and day of bitter anguish, becomes unspeakably precious to our souls. And most especially when, by His own command, bread broken and wine outpoured remind us of the crown of thorns, and the cruel cross, and the soldier's spear, and the bleeding form of the Son of God; and when we remember that *our* sins demanded the Sacrifice, our wanderings the smiting of the Shepherd, we are touched to the heart. Were the Lord's Supper nothing more than an outward memorial, there would surely be therein enough to speak to the inmost soul of each believer, and to cause him to cry out—

"Lord, I love Thee, and adore ;
Oh, for grace to love Thee more ! "

Secondly, this is a *typical* or *figurative* ordinance.

As our bodily life is frequently used as a figure or emblem of our spiritual life, so our bodily and outward reception of nourishment is here and elsewhere considered as a type of our spiritual reception of spiritual nourishment. The partaker of the Paschal Lamb, if a religious partaker, symbolised in his participation thereof his anticipation of the coming of the true Lamb of God : thus " showing forth His death till He came." In like manner, all who rightly come to the Lord's

Table look beyond the outward memorial which they "press with their lips." The language of their hearts thus declares:—"I eat this bread and drink this wine as a remembrance of my Lord. And further, as my body is nourished by the bread and wine, so do I feed my hungry and thirsty soul on the Sacrifice, the broken Body and the outpoured Blood of Christ. His death has been for me. He was wounded for *my* transgressions, He was bruised for *my* iniquities. This supports and satisfies my soul. I partake of this Sacrifice on Calvary, and feed on Him, now my risen and living Lord, in my heart, by faith with thanksgiving."

Faith—that is, a firm belief in Christ's work for us, is the mouth, so to speak, of our souls. Thus we feed, "after a heavenly and spiritual manner," on heavenly food, and our souls are refreshed, nourished, and strengthened by the fresh appropriation of the Sacrifice of Christ, as are our bodies by the bread and wine.

There may be, and there is, constantly this inward feeding on the Body and Blood of Christ, quite separately from the outward partaking of the bread and wine. So our Lord has Himself taught us, and such we find the teaching of our Church.

In the sixth chapter of St. John we have recorded a discourse of Christ's uttered long before the institution of His ordinance of the Lord's Supper. More clearly than almost any other portion of His Word does this show in what consists the *true* feeding on His Flesh and Blood. "*I am the Bread of Life:* he that cometh to me shall never hunger; and he that believeth on Me shall never thirst."

And in this passage of our Lord's teaching, what we are very particularly to observe is the manner in which the three expressions, "*Coming,*" "*Believing,*" and "*Eating the flesh and drinking the blood*" *of Christ*, are used by Him as meaning the same thing, are interchanged the one for the other, and bear the same promises attached to them.

"He that *cometh* to Me shall never hunger."
"Him that *cometh* unto Me I will in no wise cast out."
"No man can *come* unto Me, except the Father, which hath sent Me, draw him; and I will raise him up at the last day."
"Every man that hath heard and learned of the Father *cometh* unto Me."

"This is the work of God, that ye *believe* on Him whom He hath sent."
"He that *believeth* on Me shall never thirst."
"This is the will of Him that sent Me, that every one which seeth the Son, and *believeth* on Him, may have everlasting life: and I will raise him up at the last day."
"He that *believeth* on Me hath everlasting life."

"Except ye *eat the flesh* of the Son of Man, and *drink His blood*, ye have no life in you."
"Whoso *eateth My flesh*, and *drinketh My blood*, hath eternal life, and I will raise him up at the last day. For My flesh is meat indeed, and my blood is drink indeed."
"He that *eateth My flesh*, and *drinketh My blood*, dwelleth in Me and I in him."

Thus, and in the ensuing verses, did our great

Teacher, in a three-fold form of words, leave to us the mighty doctrine that unless we *come* to Him, *believe* on Him, *feed on the sacrifice at Calvary of His Flesh and Blood*, partake of Him as of that alone which can satisfy the longing soul, and fill the hungry soul with goodness, we have no life in us. And, still further to make clear to His people that this feeding is the purely spiritual act of faith, the laying hold on, and appropriation of, Christ, the Bread of God, as their Substitute and Sin-offering, He gave, as it were, a postscript to that solemn discourse: "The words that I speak unto you, they are spirit and they are life."

The Church of England repeats this Scriptural doctrine, that there may be the spiritual participation in the Body and Blood of Christ without the outward sign accompanying. For we find in the Rubric for the Office of the Communion of the Sick:—

"If any man, ... by any just impediment, do not receive the Sacrament of Christ's Body and Blood, the Curate shall instruct him that *if he do truly repent him of his sins, and steadfastly believe that Jesus Christ has suffered death upon the Cross for him, and shed His Blood for his redemption, earnestly remembering the benefits he hath thereby, and giving him hearty thanksgiving therefore, he doth eat and drink the Body and Blood of Christ profitably to his soul's health, although he do not receive the Sacrament with his mouth.*"

But there may be, and there is, too frequently, the *outward* partaking of the ordinance of the Lord's Supper without any real or spiritual participation in the food of Christ's Body and Blood.

Of this St. Paul wrote, 1 Cor. xi. 29, when warning men against unworthy participation. The Corinthians had made the Lord's Table a place of gluttony and drunkenness; they had brought carnal and sensual appetites to a holy ordinance, and were thus warned: —" Whosoever shall eat this bread, and drink this cup of the Lord, unworthily, shall be guilty of the body and blood of the Lord. . . . . He that eateth and drinketh unworthily, eateth and drinketh condemnation* to himself, not discerning the Lord's body." Any careless or profane approach to the Lord's Table is a setting at nought of the sacrifice which is there commemorated. Any resting in the mere *outward* ordinance, without the inward participation in that which it sets forth, brings condemnation to him who thus blindly draws near, " not discerning the Lord's body" behind the lattice-work of the emblems. " He that *seeth* the Son, and believeth on Him, hath everlasting life." To this effect, also, is the teaching of the Catechism, which tells us that true repentance and living faith are required of those who would come to the Lord's Supper.

Thirdly, we must look upon this ordinance, not as a sign merely, but as another of the *means of grace* provided in the wilderness by the Lord of the Pilgrims.

* Such is the truer rendering of the word damnation in 1 Cor. xi. 29.

A believing approach to God through Christ is ever met by a loving drawing near of God to our souls. The Prodigal Son, when yet "a great way off," was met by his father. "Draw nigh unto God, and He will draw nigh unto you," is the exhortation of the Apostle. And the reason is laid open to us by our Lord:—" No man *can* come unto Me except the Father which hath sent Me draw him." Such an approach is very specially that which we make at the Table of the Lord; when low at His feet, we tell Him that the burden of our sins is intolerable, and cling to His work of atonement as our only hope. There do we hear Him say, "Go in peace, thy sins are forgiven thee: thy faith hath saved thee." We see in the pierced hands and wounded side of our crucified Lord—in His Body broken and His Blood outpoured—the full assurance of our penalty having been paid in His person, and realise the truth of His promise, " Where two or three are gathered together in My Name, there am I in the midst of them."

Our Heavenly Master's own command that we should thus meet in remembrance of Him, is another assurance to our souls that He will there communicate to us of His grace. And, further, the subject is enlarged upon by St. Paul, where he tells us that " the cup of blessing which we bless is the communion" (or partaking uniting us to Christ) " of the blood of Christ, and the bread which we break the communion of the body of Christ" (1 Cor. x. 16), which verse forms a link of a very close argument wherein the Apostle, having pointed out how, in the history of the golden calf, the Israelites, after having eaten before God of the peace-offerings, which showed forth Christ's death sacrificially till He came, "rose up to play" (that is, to idolatrous and indecent dancing), warns the Corinthians that they should avoid every semblance of taking part in idolatrous worship as inconsistent with their having at the Lord's Table in like manner eaten of sacred emblems which, as memorials, also showed forth Christ's death, and in receiving which they spiritually fed on His Body and Blood, and thus were joined to Him, and He to them.

And as every ordinance of Christ's appointing must be to the soul of all who rightly receive it a channel of His grace,—" a means whereby we receive the same,"—so likewise does the experience of each believing communicant testify to his having found the Lord's Supper to be such to his soul. "He filleth the hungry with good things." He washes the stains from our soiled garments, and sends us forth cleansed by His blood; yea, he puts on us the best robe, and reminds us of the unsearchable riches of His grace, and bids us think even now of our betrothal to Him in righteousness, and that we are even here bone of His bone and flesh of His flesh,—one in Him and He in us.

Fourthly, *the communion of saints* is here peculiarly realised and enjoyed; since all, being partakers of that spiritual bread, even the Body of Christ, recognise that, being members of that Body, they are one in Him. "We being many are one bread and one body: for we are all partakers of that one bread. "Now ye are the body of Christ, and members in particular."

The Supper of the Lord is indeed "a sign of the love that Christians ought to have among themselves one to another." Its speaking emblems repeat His lesson, "A new commandment I give unto you; as I have loved you, that ye also love one another." The whole ordinance, bidding us realise our unity with Christ, reminds us further that "whether one member suffer, all the members suffer with it; or one member rejoice, all the members rejoice with it." Never, perhaps, so forcibly as at the Table of our Lord do His people realise the love which He would have them bear the one to the other,—

"Here do we abide in union
With each other and the Lord;
And possess in sweet communion
Joys which earth cannot afford."

Fifthly, and very specially, this is an *anticipative* ordinance.

"Ye do show forth the Lord's death '*till He come.*'" It points forward to the glory which shall be revealed when, according to His promise at its institution, the

Son of Man shall drink the fruit of the vine new with us in His Father's kingdom. Here, burdened with sin and infirmity, we kneel at the Table of the Lord: but there, in unsullied purity and in the glory of the resurrection life, we shall attend on Him without distraction. Here our union with Him is invisible, and often difficult of realization; but there, as the Bride, the Lamb's wife, we shall be visibly joined to Him in perfect oneness, and amid the anthems of countless saints. Here we behold a Saviour crucified, humiliated, bruised for our iniquities; but there we shall see Him as he is in the glory of the Father, risen for our justification, having the pre-eminence, the Head over all things to the Church, which is His Body, the fulness of Him that filleth all in all.

We would earnestly advise the enlarging in simple and easy language upon this five-fold view of the Lord's Supper, as of essential importance in giving to candidates for admission to the Communion clear and definite views concerning its import and preciousness. So thick a haze has been permitted to surround an ordinance in its perfect simplicity speaking with power to the humblest and least educated believer in Christ, that the teacher cannot be too solicitous in clearing it away, and in setting forth the Divine teaching concerning it, from which all human superstitions must be withdrawn.

His next course will be to take up, one by one, the various excuses which keep too many from this high privilege.

"I am too sinful."

"I am afraid I don't love the Lord."

"I am afraid of falling back after."

All these, and many others, he will show to be the very reasons for bringing the humble and contrite to the Feast, where, in most constraining power, the love of Christ and His willingness to forgive "to the uttermost" are shown forth.

Does the hungry man refuse the banquet because he is so hungry?

Does the poor man refuse riches because of his poverty?

Does the sick man refuse the healing draught because of his sickness nigh unto death?

Hunger, poverty, disease—these are the very grounds upon which his claims are urged. He pleads them as those which entitle him to assistance, and he obtains relief.

And so the hungry come to Christ, the Bread of Life, to be filled; and the poverty-stricken to the King at His Table to be made rich; and the sin-sick souls to the great High Priest who hath suffered, being tempted, to be made whole.

Concerning *preparation for the Lord's Supper*,—a subject abundantly large enough for a separate chapter,—our space forbids lengthened suggestions. The following words, however, from the letters of the late Rev. H. Venn, should be engraven upon the heart and memory of every one who would draw near with the hope of obtaining real benefit to his soul:—"I find with regard to myself that the benefit of Prayers, Sacraments, and the means of grace, bears exact proportion to the care I take to implore the influence and operation of the Spirit in them; that when I am only a little concerned in asking of the Lord the inestimable comfort of His help, my spiritual duties afford me little comfort in the exercise, and leave no lasting impressions. On the contrary, when I am importunate with the Lord to put life and power in the ordinances, and to make me feel some correspondent affections, I am enabled to say, 'Truly our fellowship is with the Father, and with His Son Jesus Christ.'" In these words we have the true nature of preparation for every spiritual exercise—the diligent seeking for the Holy Spirit's help that in divinely-appointed outward ordinances our souls may find and enjoy communion with the Lord of ordinances. And such must be the preparation of those who desire in faith to draw near to the Table of the Lord.

As the human tendency is ever to take from the

simplicity of God's appointments by adding thereto doctrines and commandments of men, so the subject of preparation for the Lord's Supper has been frequently put forward in a most mistaken point of view. This preparation has been represented as requiring that, in prospect of the approaching solemnity, men should transfer themselves into an entirely distinct state of religious feeling and devotion from that of their ordinary life; and, day by day, mount, by prayers, meditations, and vows of obedience, upon a species of spiritual ladder which shall finally land them upon a platform of sanctification sufficiently exalted to permit of their fitly receiving the Holy Sacrament.

The utter contradiction which this system of preparation offers to every page of the Word of God appears upon the slightest comparison of the two. "The preparations of the heart are *from the Lord*," and the Holy Spirit can alone, by His influences from on high, and by the application of the Blood of Christ, meetly fit us for appearing before Him. An endeavour to lay in a stock of our own merits, of vows of obedience, and of a certain registered number of hours of meditation which may be presented before Him in whose sight the heavens are not clean, as constituting a ground of acceptance, is a practical putting aside of One who, by His full, perfect, and sufficient atonement for our sins, proclaimed Himself " *the* Way."

"Let a man examine himself, and so let him eat of that bread and drink of that cup." Thus wrote the Apostle. Examination as to our being *in the faith*, as to our *repentance* for the past, as to our earnest desire for the washing away in the blood of Christ of past sin, and for grace to lead a life of more diligent holiness, will be the fit and only right accompaniments to the supplications for a blessing. A summary for self-examination and lowly preparation of heart for the Lord's Table is furnished by the beautiful words in our Service:

"Ye that do truly and earnestly repent of your sins, and are in love and charity with your neighbours, and intend to lead a new life, following the commandments of God, and walking from henceforth in His holy ways; Draw near with faith, and take this holy Sacrament for your comfort."

The last portion of the instruction given to intending communicants will probably be best conveyed by a continuous explanation of the Service itself, in course of which the teacher will naturally draw attention to many points dwelt upon in the previous course of teaching. And surely it will not be without finding his own heart warmed by the tender sacredness of an ordinance more closely endeared to the believer by each successive observance, that he will seek to kindle in his hearers a love for the lofty Liturgy with which we celebrate our Christian Passover.

It remains only to suggest, as on former occasions, one or two plans found efficacious in helping members of the Bible-class to regard the habit of regular communion in the light of a serious duty as well as of a high privilege.

It is found well on the Sunday before to echo the invitation given in church, and to entreat each one to consider it during the week as solemnly and earnestly conveyed to himself. A few minutes' address upon the subject, showing forth affectionately and simply the greatness of the love which has extended it, and the solemnity of their danger who habitually live in disregard of the Lord's command, will be well bestowed. And the teacher may take the opportunity of inviting to some private conversation with himself those who are divided in their minds between the desire of accepting the privilege offered and the fear lest they should come unworthily.

Another plan, found to be attended with much benefit is that of a short meeting on the Friday or Saturday evening before, for all who are to attend at the Lord's Table on the Sunday. These meetings, uniting in brotherly love, and in peculiarly close association, those members of the Bible-class who have really known for themselves the Christ, the Saviour of the world, have often been times of special blessing. The teacher has joined with the class in earnest prayer and confession, and in distinct supplication for the Lord's presence and nearness on occasion of meeting Him at His Table in obedience to his own command; and some special promise, from His own Word, has been agreed upon for meditation previous to, and at the time of, the administration of the Communion. A gathering like this tends to refresh and to re-awaken to a sense of the sacredness of communion privilege the regular communicants of the class, as well as the teacher himself; while the impression upon those who may have only recently been led to consider the duty and happiness of attendance is often serious and lasting. "Such hymns as, " When I survey the wondrous cross;" " I lay my sins on Jesus;" "Just as I am;" "We love Thee, Lord;" " Jesu, refuge of my soul;" and others specially appropriate, have, as softly sung by all assembled, touched many a heart, and brought peace to more than one attendant at such an ante-sacramental meeting.

The last suggestion we would offer is concerning the importance of strengthening the sense of the privileges belonging to attendance at the Lord's Table, by making the recurrence of some special Church festival the occasion of an annual gathering of past and present members of the Bible-class. New Year's Day, Easter, Whit Sunday, Christmas Day, may, in different places, and among different classes, have, respectively, their peculiar advantages. In some Bible-classes Easter Sunday is the day of such joyful union. Old members come from miles off to join with their former teachers and friends in keeping the Feast, while to the teacher falls the pleasant duty of arranging for their rest and refreshment after service, and even, when some have come in from the country, for their being housed from Saturday to Monday. All sit together in church; and few more joyful notes swell the strain of gladness than the burst of praise in which so many well-known voices unite—" Christ our Passover is sacrificed for us; therefore let us keep the Feast!" There has, on some of these occasions, been a goodly gathering at the Bible-class afterwards—the old Christian greeting of Easter morning, "*The Lord is risen!*" being exchanged from one to another. Some hymn or chorus, specially prepared for the day, is always sung; and, having been previously printed on separate sheets, is given as a memorial to those who leave.

Amid all the discouragements, the anxieties, and the self-denials of his work, seasons like these are surely intended to bring to the earnest teacher special rejoicing, with a peculiar consciousness of his being permitted to be a "worker together with God." And while kneeling from time to time at the spot where not unfrequently it has seemed as though "the confines of earth touched the borders of heaven," the sense of his weakness, and the need of grace sufficient for his own wants, and for those of the little number with whom he is so nearly associated, will lead him to a fresh confidence and trust in a Love undying, and there evidently set forth. And, with the sense of the reality of the High Priest's entrance into the Most Holy Place to offer for us His own Blood, and His spotless merits he will look for and expect the benediction from the Lord Himself:—

> "Thy pardoning love possessing,
> Our doubts and fears shall cease;
> *We are waiting for the blessing,
> O bid us go in peace!*"

CHAPTER IX.

ON BIBLE-CLASS FESTIVALS.

WITH the conviction that a short chapter on Bible-class festivals should find a place in this volume, we venture to offer to our readers a few suggestions which may be of value as the result of manifold experiences both as regards the difficulties and the pleasures accompanying their organisation.

We will leave on one side the comparatively easy question of summer excursions and garden festivities —occasions on which Nature takes her full share of responsibility in the entertainment of the guests, and carries out the object better than most of us; turning at present to the wintry side of the picture, and endeavouring, so far as it may be in our power, to answer the not unfrequent, and often somewhat desponding inquiry concerning the guests under consideration, "But what will you do with them when they come?"

With reference, then, to a Christmas or New Year's gathering of Bible-class members, our first suggestion would be as to securing a room of large and capable dimensions. Some school-room can generally be found fully spacious enough for an ordinary Bible-class tea-party: its organisers probably agreeing with us in the assertion that freedom of intercourse and an absence of *gêne* or restraint, are almost impossibilities when the guests can scarcely move without begging each other's pardon, and have a consciousness throughout the evening of being under the close and immediate inspection of their superiors in position. We have heard of some ladies who have shown their kind feeling for Bible-classes of milliners and dress-makers by receiving them annually in their own drawing-rooms: but, though such a reception would undoubtedly be felt a high honour, we question whether anything like the same enjoyment can be got out of an apartment of which the Brussels carpets and pier-glasses would inevitably call for "company manners," as out of a roomy and well-lit school-room, the long tables and boarded floors suggesting easy sociality of intercourse, with opportunities for breaking up into little knots for aside chats and for greetings of old friends.

We would decorate our rooms, and make the decorations matter of interest and admiration. Should texts be interwoven with evergreens, we would suggest that they should be *season* texts, Christmas or New Year mottoes, likely to stamp the joy of the season on the whole festival. We need hardly say a word as to the taste of putting up mottoes such as we heard of on one occasion—" The rich and the poor meet together; the Lord is the Maker of them all."

Then, as to the manner of reception: we would suggest to teachers, and to all who assist as superintendents or otherwise, that the little attention of receiving Bible-class guests, not in out-door, but in in-door attire, brightened by some slight festal touches, is not thrown away. It helps to carry out the feeling of the occasion being one honoured and regarded with pleasure by the givers of the entertainment as well as by the invited Bible-class members. In one such gathering we noticed that every lady-friend helping in the arrangements wore a bow of white ribbon; while little nosegays, presented in more than one instance to their teacher by the Bible-class members themselves, gave an idea of pleasant preparation for the evening. We do not receive friends of our own standing, in hats and bonnets; and we can imagine that the vision of a teacher's familiar Sunday bonnet might convey to her class an indistinct feeling of being regarded as only on a footing to be received professionally—the very notion which we desire to avoid.

In many towns kindly-disposed nursery gardeners are

to be found who will lend flowering plants or evergreens for the white-covered tables. These, placed at regular intervals, lend something of the æsthetic to the more practical provision of cake and of the tempting loaves and golden butter; for bread and butter should not, to our thinking, be cut up and piled—school fashion— on these occasions.

Let us suppose the visitors assembled. The Bible-class guests, mingling with such former members as, in consequence of previous efforts on the part of the teachers, may have been enabled to attend, are received by that pleasant little congregational alliance which, with the clergyman at its head, includes Bible-class and Sunday-school teachers, some of the working ladies and gentlemen of the parish, it may be, the schoolmaster and mistress, and a small general following of helpers in various positions, without whom no such festivity is ever supposed to be properly organised. There is care as to the grouping of old friends at the tea-tables; and shy new-comers, at "the tea-party" for the first time, are introduced by the teacher to kindly longer-established members, with the understanding that they shall thus be made to feel at home with the others. The signal for silence is given, and grace is either said by the clergyman or sung by all present.

Then it is that a little tact will be required on the

part of presiding friends, in order to the breaking through of a certain amount of ice—a shy feeling of constraint—which, unless quickly done away with, is fatal to any real enjoyment on the part of the guests. We hope that our readers will not think it derogatory to the dignity of their office, if we suggest that some quiet fun, freely promoted at this stage of the proceedings, will not by any means interfere with more serious engagements later on in the evening. We have seen the tongues of a whole table untied by the propounding of a riddle with some mirthful answer; and as we take it for granted that at each table assistant friends will be engaged in taking, as well as in making, tea with the rest of the party, they will find the advice to provide themselves with a few queries of this nature, ready to be launched at suitable intervals, by no means to be despised.

After tea, games are generally popular. Magic music —if a piano or concertina, with a good performer, can be secured—is an excellent amusement, and highly appreciated. The person selected for finding a hidden article, or for performing some prescribed action, should be sufficiently well known, and able to enter with humour into the spirit of the game. Proverbs, magic words, and such games, admit of a great deal of enjoyment; and sometimes really good dissolving views, or a clever conjuror, will keep a whole party entranced for a great part of the evening. We have known the latter exhibition wind up brilliantly with the mysterious hat, from which some little gift has been produced for each person present.

On one occasion of a Christmas gathering, much and prolonged interest and pleasure was excited by the delivery at the door, after a resounding postman's knock, of a parcel of letters, duly stamped, one of which was directed, in an unknown hand, to each member of the party, teachers included. The first surprise was followed by no little laughter, and by cries of "A trick!" when it was discovered that each envelope contained a perfectly blank sheet of paper; while all sorts of surmises were indulged in as to the perpetrator of the not very brilliant hoax. The affair seemed to have passed off, when the sender of the letters—the only person in the secret—declaring aloud that her hands were too cold for music until she had warmed them at the fire, proceeded rather noticeably to do so, her own blank letter in her hand. The next minute she exclaimed that the paper was covered with writing. There was, of course, a general cry for the development of each of the other letters; and, as one by one these were held to the fire or the lamps, and read aloud by some of the gentlemen present, the invisible ink* was made clearly visible, and each one found her-

* Invisible ink may be obtained at any stationer's. The whitest paper should be used for such letters.

self possessed of some appropriate Christmas greeting in verse, or of some other little written remembrance of the evening—compositions from which a sparkle of humour was by no means excluded, and which were carried off as treasured memorials of a festivity afterwards described by a poor woman as having been "just like heaven!"

Photographic albums, containing the portraits of past and present members of the Bible-class, are much in request on such occasions, as well as others with likenesses of the clergymen and their families, Sunday-school teachers, and other well-known friends. We would advise every teacher to possess a Bible-class album, which all will take pleasure in furnishing.

Music and singing should form, to our thinking, a prominent portion of the pleasures of an assembly such as we are describing. Probably there will have been previous practising for the occasion, and the sweet voices of Bible-class singers, past and present, will be united in old songs, as well as in others more recently acquired. It will be found a good plan to have a few songs specially belonging, as it were, to an individual Bible-class, and yearly sung at such meetings. Absent members will be recalling them with loving memories, and they will acquire a sort of sacredness as time goes on, and as one and another who may have formerly joined in them falls out of the ranks,—it may be to join in a better song above. One such song, which, in a Bible-class of many years' standing, is what the "Dulce domum" might be to a Winchester scholar, has been appended, in the belief that some teachers may be glad at the new-year season to adopt it for those under their charge.

The music should not, we are inclined to suggest, be wholly confined to the class singers. It is no small pleasure when a little instrumental music—a duet, it may be, of harp or concertina and piano—is performed by some of their entertainers, or when some glee or chorus, demanding more educated voices, is contributed by ladies and gentlemen sufficiently interested in the evening's success thus to lend their aid.

Music is an excellent medium for shading off from the games, from gift-distributions, from the Christmas-tree, or from other more lively pleasures of the evening, to the more serious tone of thought and feeling which should mark its conclusion; and as gleeful Christmas or New Year songs gradually give place to carol, hymn, or anthem, the minds of all will be insensibly prepared for a closing address, and for evening prayer, conducted, it is to be hoped, by one of the clergymen of the parish. How valuable and how earnest such addresses may be it is beyond our province to show; but all who have followed us so far with somewhat of sympathetic feeling will understand the longing desire on the part of the teacher that such an address should more closely link the class to its pastor, and should be a fit carrying on, not only of the uniting and gladdening influences of the occasion, but also of the constant endeavours, in the weekly instruction, to set forth the necessity for a personal union with a crucified and living Saviour.

When all guests have departed, and the closing refreshments have been handed round, the teacher, who will have contrived to gain many an aside talk during the evening, should, if possible, have a last few minutes alone with the members of the Bible-class— making it the occasion of expressing greetings, and hopes, and interest, for which, in the case of many of the old members, there may not be a later opportunity. There will, probably, be a short review of the Bible-class history of the past year, a few words as to increase or decrease in numbers, as to attendance at the Lord's Table, as to advance, or the reverse, in missionary effort. There will be remembrance of absent members, and, it may be, of some gathered to a better Home; and, after a special renewal of welcome to old friends and associates who may have been able to attend on the occasion, some short, earnest word or motto for the coming year will, probably, at such a time sink into the hearts of all present. Perhaps the sweet notes of " May the grace of Christ our Saviour " will form a last harmony, closing in the evening's enjoyment.

Such gatherings, passing though they be, tend in no slight measure to the building up into a real and solid fabric Bible-Class influences and associations. The Review, although it may not seem a military measure of aggressive importance, tells in no insignificant degree on the standing and spirit of the regiment. It is our own fault if *our* Reviews fail to do the same.

A HAPPY NEW YEAR.

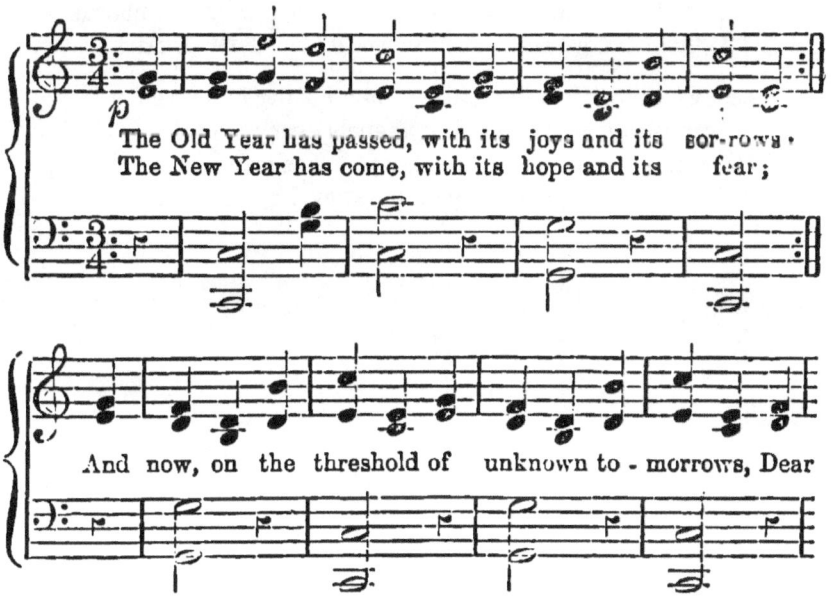

The Old Year has passed, with its joys and its sor-rows
The New Year has come, with its hope and its fear;

And now, on the threshold of unknown to - morrows, Dear

ON BIBLE-CLASS FESTIVALS.

friends, we would wish you A HAPPY NEW YEAR.

We ask not for honour, we look not for treasure;
  These last but a moment—they soon disappear;
Though ours were silver and gold without measure,
  Oh, *these* could not bring us A HAPPY NEW YEAR!

We know not what cares may e'en now be before us,
  We know not what joy or what grief may be near;
We know not which voice may be missed from our chorus
  When next we shall wish you A HAPPY NEW YEAR!

But we know that the smile of our Father in heaven
  Brings sunshine to sorrow, dispels every fear:
He will not withhold who a Saviour has given,
  And oh, may *He* send you A HAPPY NEW YEAR!

[*This hymn may be obtained separately.*]

CHAPTER X.

BIBLE-CLASS CORRESPONDENCE.

"I HAVE no greater joy than to hear that my children walk in the truth." So wrote the beloved disciple to one of his children in the Lord, of whom, even in days when communication by letter was no easy matter, he had never lost sight. And in studying the New Testament and the conduct of the Apostles towards those over whom they had been placed, we cannot but be struck with their determination to keep up by correspondence fellowship with those from whom they were parted, as well as by their expectation of real results in the hearts and lives of their distant flocks from the study of Epistles carefully drawn up, and constantly followed by prayer. St. John, whether writing to the elect lady concerning her children, and those to whom she might open her house, or to Gaius in affectionate commendation of his hospitality, showed forth that individual interest in the affairs of his friends which we all know how to prize. And yet more, St. Paul, who in his Epistles to the churches never forgot *remembrance by name* of those whom such remembrance would, he well knew, cheer and inspirit in their work, conducting his correspondence with a view to its exercising the greatest possible amount of influence, wrote to the Colossians, "When this Epistle is read among you, cause that it be read in the church of the Laodiceans, and that ye likewise read the Epistle from Laodicea." In all cases he displayed that individual care and recollection of the men and women who laboured in the Lord, which must have in no small degree enhanced his personal influence, and must have caused them to realise that "though absent in body he was with them in spirit, joying and beholding their order, and the steadfastness of their faith in Christ."

And we who are teachers, though not Apostles, have it as our office to hand on, and to impress, and to labour to disseminate apostolic teaching; and it surely becomes us well, taking an example from their practice, to leave no means unused whereby we may more widely and effectually extend the influence of our instructions. Our letters to those separated from us by absence are not, indeed, to be ranked in importance with inspired epistles; but it is for us to remember that the Holy Spirit's guidance, and power to give us a right judgment in all things, is a present and living reality; and that He will never refuse to direct us in efforts for which His teaching has been sought, or withhold from them that blessing which can infuse life into the simplest letters written for the Master's sake.

We imagine it impossible that any earnest teacher can be insensible to the importance of a system of correspondence by which he or she may maintain relations with those separated from the influence of the Bible-class. One of its appurtenances should always be a register containing the names and addresses of former members, together with the date of their leaving the class; and when the numbers of the class are large, such a register will demand revision as names become changed by marriage, and addresses need alteration. The existence of this register should be known in the class; valuable aid towards the maintenance of its accuracy being often furnished by its members who know that the teacher is glad to be informed of changes of name and place, and who, mindful of their absent associates, will frequently stay behind with some request such as, "I've heard from Mary, ma'am; and she's gone to a new place, and she told me to give her duty to you, and to say how much she misses the class on Sundays; and I think, ma'am, she'd be very glad if you'd write to her. She didn't *tell* me to say so, but I've brought you her address, as I know she'd feel shy of writing to you first."

If these pages should by any chance be studied by teachers who have not been led to regard correspondence with former members of their classes as a part of their duty, it will hardly be out of place here to impress upon them the wide department of possible usefulness upon which they may thus enter. How many of us who have known for ourselves loneliness, sickness, depression, or indecision as to our path of duty, have looked out for, and eagerly grasped, the letter for which we had hoped—perhaps even prayed—the letter from some dear absent friend or relative to whom we have learnt to look up with reverent affection, assuring us of sympathy and of constant remembrance. Have not the kind words leading us to look on the bright side of our trouble, and, above all, helping us with some fresh thought concerning a present Love, and a realised and living Saviour, been sometimes regarded as a message of help and guidance received directly from His own hand?

But, keenly as we may for ourselves have felt the comfort and help of such communications, we can, perhaps, hardly realise how precious to some serving sisters or brothers, with hardly any one else to write to them, and for the first time, it may be, absent from their own homes, a letter from a teacher to whom they have attached themselves may prove.

"I was standing all alone on Christmas-eve," wrote

one such, "and feeling so low, away in London, and thinking about everybody at dear St. M——'s, and how busy you would be, and how happy I used to be there when Christmas came round, and it *did* seem so lonely. And while I was there, looking out of the window, the postman came to the door, and I went for the letters, and there was yours to me. It made everything seem different to think I was remembered; and your sending me the songs they were to sing in the schools brought all our St. M——'s Christmas hymns and songs to my mind, and I seemed to feel myself there once more, with the thought that in all of it you hadn't forgotten me."

Surely one such testimony from a young servant in her first place to a teacher seeking to follow her out with love and prayer, would be an encouragement to the adoption of a plan often involving effort and self-denial, but almost more than any other productive of a rich harvest of at least grateful appreciation. Those who for any length of time have carried out such efforts, will be able to quote innumerable instances in which such testimonies as, "Just when I needed help, your kind letter came as a message to me;" "I was reading over your letter that you wrote to me last New Year, now that I'm in such trouble, and I know that you won't think me taking a liberty to ask you to tell me what I should do;" "I never come to Sunday afternoon when the Bible-class is meeting, without trying to be with you in spirit, and praying for a blessing,"—bring a present affluence of encouragement to the teacher in the assurance that this department of his labour is not in vain in the Lord.

Besides the actual teaching which letters such as a wise and loving teacher will send to his class friends ought to convey, and beyond the cheering sense of being remembered, which would in itself be enough to cause them to be hailed with joy by those to whom they are addressed, the sense of being regarded as a correspondent by a former teacher, the assurance that in all times of difficulty, doubt, and bereavement a few lines to a tried friend of superior education and position will bring a prompt answer of sympathy and affectionate guidance, will often infuse, and at all times strengthen, a feeling of self-respect, raising and ennobling the character which from such stepping-stones will most frequently rise to reverence. And this sense of sympathy, this belief that what touches him is actually for that reason of importance to his teacher, that he is remembered, thought of, talked of, prayed for, will, not unfrequently, even in the absence of a higher motive, elevate the heart of a former hearer; while the resolution flashes in upon him to live and work "so as that they shall see it isn't being thrown away having such as cares to think of me when I'm gone."

When the attendance at a Bible-class is, and has been, numerous, a frequent correspondence with its absent members is, of course, an impossibility. In many cases it is enough that they should, on occasion of the parting interview, and after the parting prayer with their teacher, be told that at any time, when needing help, or desiring a letter, they have but to write, and they may be sure of an answer. The request that they will themselves write, on finding out how they like their new position, will often furnish them with a pretext for a first letter, the teacher's reply to which will be abundantly sufficient to reassure them as to the affectionate reception of any subsequent epistle. Then, when sickness comes, or when seeking a situation, or when needing help, they will have the comfort of knowing that an experiment which succeeded before will be successful again, and they will have learnt to turn to a tried friend without fear of being misunderstood.

Concerning an annual letter to the whole class we shall add a few words further on. But we would at this point pause for a moment at the enquiry made by some teachers less experienced in this matter than those who have long been in the work, who have been heard to exclaim, "Don't you find it hard to write to those sort of people? I should hardly know how to begin or what to say to persons of that class. I should be very glad to give them any pleasure I could; but I really cannot see that unless they were ill, or in some great trouble, I should find anything particular to write about."

We are inclined to think that the fact of being a teacher at all argues the existence of so much sympathy and kind Christian feeling that most of our fraternity, fairly determined to make a beginning, would find the act of placing themselves in their correspondents' position, and fancying what would suit them best in that position, a sufficient starting-point for a letter certain to convey unaffected pleasure. But might we venture to offer one or two suggestions on the subject, the first would be this:—Do not be afraid of lowering your dignity by writing to the lad behind the counter, or to this girl in service, or to that young person in business, as you would write to a friend in your own position. Write naturally, kindly, we might add, *respectfully*; by which we mean that a cordial respect for the position of honourable bread-winning and self-reliant occupation should be transparent through all you write. Our dignity can take care of itself. To *write down* to your Bible-class friend would be as little likely to do him good as talking from a pedestal of superior position would be likely to reach his heart. We would not compose a letter like a sermon, as if religion were the only ground on which friends of different positions could meet. A little chat concerning the teacher's own interests and occupations, implying a genuine confidence in the sympathy of the reader, a notice of any family changes, a few words about the interest of the parish or district, such as would be pleasant for an absent one to hear, will convince him that you do not only write, as it were, professional letters, but that you write as from one friend to another. It need hardly be added that a notice of any intercourse with members of his family, —how they looked, and "how much they thought of him,"—will, in case of its having come to pass, be warmly appreciated; nor, further, that the teacher will so throw himself into his correspondent's occupations, position, and difficulties, as to make him feel that each of these have been real matters of consideration with him, and are fully entered into. There will then, probably, be some little notice of the Bible-class, of increase of numbers, of old friends who have left the place, and of new plans started. And we can imagine some such words as the following introducing the earnest concluding portion of the letter:—

"We all miss you, dear C——, and wish for you on Sundays; and we all look forward to having you with us again. I was thinking of you particularly last Sunday afternoon, for you would have enjoyed our subject. It was ——,"—and here, perhaps, the chief point of the lesson, the parting motto and a few helpful lasting thoughts will be given, which will make the letter one to be laid aside, and read and re-read, Bible in hand.

Some little enclosure will peculiarly enhance the value of the letter, and the sense of the friendliness which has dictated it. Photographs are invaluable for this purpose, while a small illuminated text, or a well-selected hymn-leaflet, or a few flowers, will be prized far more than the inexperienced reader can imagine. "I counted all the letters you ever wrote to me, last week," we heard one young mother say to her teacher, eight or nine years after she had left the Bible-class; "they came to near fifty. I wouldn't lose one of them not for anything."

Often by thus keeping in sight those who have long left the place and the class, opportunities for meeting on journeys, and on occasion of visits from home, will present themselves; and few pleasanter interludes can diversify a travelling expedition than the sight at some wayside station of an old Bible-class friend who, it may be, has "married away in the country," and who, with some bonny baby in her arms, is proud to meet the train to gain the chance of a few minutes with her old teacher.

Another advantage of thus following out members of a Bible-class is the opportunity afforded of introducing them to some kindred class, or to some friend of clergyman in the locality to which they have removed. Surely no teacher having it in his power to give to one of his flock going to a strange place an introduction by which a kind and Christian friend might be secured, would omit to avail himself of such an opportunity. Let him fancy himself placed amongst strangers, and cut off from home associations, and he will realise how greatly such an introduction would be valued. It is, indeed, much to be desired that, with this object in view, some list of adult classes, male and female, throughout the kingdom, in which a line of introduction might secure a welcome to a stranger from a kindred Bible-class, might be in the hands of every Bible-class teacher. Such an organization, while it would tend, by the fact of enrolment amongst others, to prevent a sense of isolation in the work common to many teachers, would be, further, an invaluable resource to those who, earnest for the welfare of souls committed to their charge, might at once transfer them to a centre of Christian influence and care.

"Parted from E. and her sister. I never felt more pain in wishing good-bye to any members of the Bible-class. They know the truth intellectually better than any, and are, so far as I can judge, strangers to any real desire after change of heart." Such, several years ago, was the entry in the private journal of a Bible-class which has furnished many of the experiences recorded in these chapters. The young women alluded to were old acquaintances; the elder, a handsome, stylishly-dressed dressmaker; the younger, an apprentice in a house of business. They were going to set up for themselves in London, and, doubtful as to whether they would have time to call, their teacher herself called on them to say good-bye. They were clever, superior young women, more highly educated than most of the Bible-class, and in their manners and address conveying a consciousness of capability and self-reliance likely to carry them on successfully in their new position. Their teacher was courteously and respectfully received. The young women were grateful to her for having taken the trouble of calling; and though Miss ——, the elder, was interrupted more than once by calls to the show-room, a few earnest words respecting the danger of resting for salvation on a life of mere respectability, were silently and not impatiently received.

"And now, dear friends, I want you to make me a promise before we part. I will give you an introduction to the lady at the head of a Bible-class for young persons in business. If you receive an invitation from her, will you join it? will you do it because it is my parting wish?"

The young women looked at each other. The elder did not like to bind herself; neither liked to contradict the friend whom they had known for so many years. "Well, I don't mind if we do—at least to try," was the answer at last. "Yes, ma'am, we will."

The Superintendent of the Young Women's Home in M—— Street kindly lost no time in calling on the sisters, even before they were fully established in their West-end business. She died shortly after; but her loving promptitude in acting upon the request then made to her was to bear rich fruit. She invited them to the Sunday-class, and, mindful of their promise, they came on two successive Sundays.

"I'll not trouble to come again," said the elder of the two to her sister, as they left the house; "it's dull work coming Sunday after Sunday to be preached to."

"But you know we promised Miss ——," was the answer; "it won't seem like keeping a promise to stop after only twice coming."

"Well, I'll come once more," replied the elder sister; "I'm sure three times will be keeping our word quite enough."

And on that third Sunday the class was taken by a lady whose words went home to the hearts of the sisters as no other words had ever done before. It was the beginning of life to both hearts. Soon after, a letter was received telling with gladness of the great change which had come to them, of a newly found Saviour, of joy and peace in believing—a letter expressing wonder and shame at the long neglect of the Gospel message, and earnestly thanking the friend who had introduced them to a place which had proved the birthplace of their souls. A short time after, late one evening, the mother of the young people—a truly Christian woman—called. She had been to see them in town, and had walked a long distance to the house of their former teacher. "I felt I must tell you myself, ma'am," she said, "of what a Sunday I had. My daughters were steady, respectable girls, but wilful and careless of the truth. And now," and the tears came quickly, "the change has come which I had almost given up hoping for. They seem quite full of the joy of having found the Lord. On Sunday we all went to church together, and, for the first time, all to the Lord's Table; and it seemed as if I had never known such happiness before."

After having thus been brought to know their Saviour, both sisters gave up all their spare time to helping forward the work of leading others to the same blessed hope. One, until her own health failed, took the chief management of a ragged school in one of the worst parts of the City; the elder, under the guidance of the lady whose teaching had been so blest to her, became for many years, and still continues, most useful among the young people of her own position, and many others; her superior education and manners peculiarly qualifying her to assist in such efforts.

Some months after the parting referred to, she unexpectedly called in the evening on the friend of her earlier days; and very uniting and joyful was the hour of Christian communion which followed.

"I hope you won't think me taking a liberty, ma'am," she said, before leaving; "but I've brought this little parcel for you; I know you're always so busy at Christmas time, making up presents—housewifes and bags—for the school children and Bible-class tea-party, and I've been collecting these pieces, and some which I had by me from old stores, which might save you trouble."

"But E., *these* are too good," was the reply; "I hardly like to take them; they are really of value, and might be of use to you for yourself;" for the store was of a liberal description.

"Thank you, ma'am," was the reply; "but you know I should never dress now as I used to—the more quiet the better. I was so pleased to think of something you *could* use that I might help in."

It was a passing remark, that concerning her dress; but any lady teacher will know how much was implied by the few words betraying such a complete change of taste and feeling. The quiet apparel, the neat shawl and bonnet, which, modestly put on, had replaced the showy stylish over-dressing, for ever laid aside, told a tale of their own; and on few names in a Bible-class register of many years ago does the teacher's eye rest with a deeper thankfulness than on those of the sisters whose departure had been previously recorded with no little pain and anxiety.

But we must leave this brief extract from the pages of Bible-class records, here inserted in illustration of the desirableness of following up and corresponding with absent members, for a final notice of a plan which has been found eminently useful, not only in stirring up to a sense of class-union, and distinctive fellowship, members in actual attendance on a Bible-class, but also in maintaining the feeling among former members, and in carrying to each one, present or absent, an earnest word of loving exhortation at a time, and in a manner, peculiarly calculated to be valued and remembered. We refer to the plan of a New Year's letter sent annually to every member of the class; the same letter, with the addition of a special paragraph, being sent by post to those on the teacher's list of former members.

It would be difficult, without risking a charge of exaggeration, to convey any idea of the value set upon such letters. Towards the close of the year members lingering behind after the class will put in special petitions for the remembrance of those concerning whose entry on its register they may be doubtful. "If you please, ma'am, there's Mrs. ——, she has been sometimes, but she's never joined regularly, and she doesn't like to now till after Christmas, for fear it may seem as if she wanted to come for the tea-party; but I know how she's hoping for a letter, and we know, ma'am, it *may* bring a blessing." Or, "I've heard from Jane; she's changed her place, and sent her address for fear she wouldn't get a letter." The constant recurrence of precautions from absent members to secure the reception of their former teacher's New Year's message shows the value attached to this practice.

As some teachers of large classes may not have thought of attempting such a plan, they may care to know that in this yearly letter, sent round by a messenger on New Year's-eve to each resident Bible-class member, a motto is suggested, which forms a sort of watchword for the year. Where the numbers of a class are so small that a teacher finds an individual letter to each within the compass of his time and capability, his thus writing privately will, of course, be the best plan of all. But as this is not usually possible, a lithograph or printed letter, the name of the person to whom it is addressed being filled up afterwards, together with the teacher's autograph signature, will be found nearly as welcome. One of the pretty New Year's or Christmas cards, now so common, will be found a pleasant addition.

Plans such as these, though often laborious, and demanding no little expenditure of time and care, bring good to the promoters as well as to those for whose special benefit they are undertaken. Can we write to our classes concerning the necessity for holiness of life, for daily striving, for urgent prayer, for conformity to the image of Jesus, and not have impressed upon our own hearts the earnest need of increased efforts after holiness, of renewed and constant supplication for the Holy Spirit to be shed on ourselves as well as on them? We seek to win those to whom we are closely related as brethren and friends; and assuredly we shall best be able to succeed in these efforts by constant intercourse with Him who, stooping down to our lowly humanity, whispers in our ears:—" I have called you friends; ye have not chosen Me, but I have chosen you, and ordained you, that ye should go and bring forth fruit, and that your fruit should remain; that whatsoever ye shall ask the Father, He may give it unto you."

CHAPTER XI.

ON THE BEST METHOD OF EXCITING AND MAINTAINING A MISSIONARY SPIRIT IN THE BIBLE-CLASS.

SUGGESTIONS from various quarters have led to our concluding this series of chapters with a consideration of *the best methods of interesting a Bible-class in Missionary work.*

On this subject experiences are various. One teacher suggests a Sunday in the month wholly devoted to Missionary instruction. A second considers it sufficient to superintend the monthly purchase and distribution of Missionary periodicals: while a third, perhaps, is inclined to the opinion that there is so much to be done at home, that at present foreign efforts can be left alone; and fears frightening away class-members by bringing forward the subject.

It is, of course, a matter admitting of many and various opinions; but we are inclined to think that the first of these plans, however desirable in a Sunday-school, is, in the case of a Bible-class, attended with serious drawbacks. It concentrates into one Sunday's teaching what might be with more advantage diffused, in the way of illustration, narrative, or direct instruction, through two or three; and, moreover, creates a serious break in the course of Scripture study which may be engrossing the minds of both teachers and hearers. A Bible-class attendant, deeply struck with the teacher's exposition of the conversion of St. Paul in the way to Damascus, will be hardly satisfied when, on the following Sunday, expecting the continuation of the history, he finds some Missionary narrative, however interesting, unexpectedly interrupting its course. And, indeed, the earnest teacher will feel the weekly opportunity for imparting distinctive Scriptural instruction so precious, as to grudge the dedication of so large a proportion of time exclusively to Missionary intelligence. School children have, or ought to have, daily opportunities of receiving Bible instruction; but members of the Bible-class are in general limited to those of the Sunday, which are of value accordingly. The Missionary information, also, thus delivered, will, as a general rule, be somewhat unconnected; and very frequently members who have missed the previous " Missionary afternoon," will, in consequence, find it difficult to seize on the details subsequently laid before them.

As regards the circulation of Missionary, and, indeed, of other well-certified religious periodicals, we believe it to be a plan attended with much advantage —*it being always understood that no payments are accepted by the teacher on Sunday;* but, for the arousing and maintenance in a Bible-class of real Missionary spirit, this, unaccompanied by living teaching and influence, will not, to our thinking, be of stable or permanent effect.

Holding, however, as we do, that every Church having real spiritual life must, as a necessary outgrowth of that life, be more or less a Missionary Church, and that every individual really grafted into the true Vine must, of necessity, bring forth fruit to the glory of God, it follows that a Bible-class, upon which, in smaller or greater degree, it has pleased God to pour down His Holy Spirit, must, in such degree, become a Missionary agency for the promotion of His kingdom, both at home and, so far as may be, abroad also.

"How do you contrive to get so large a Missionary collection from your Bible-class?" we heard a clergyman inquire of a teacher, as a sum of several pounds appeared in a list of yearly subscriptions.

"I ask *myself* the question," was the reply; "and I can only say ' whose hearts *the Lord* hath touched.' "

To that same class words such as these have been frequently addressed when the real mainspring of

Christian action has been dwelt upon: "It is for this reason, dear friends, that on Sundays I do not so often dwell upon things we ought or ought not to do, as upon that love of Jesus which, like a mainspring in a watch, when once ruling the heart, sets the hands and all else to work according to His will. A great many have said, 'I hope you speak to your Bible-class about the duty of dressing plainly—the young people now-a-days are ruined by the love of gay clothing!' but I cannot say that I feel inclined to do so. I would rather show you what the love of Christ is; I would rather pray for you, and entreat you, with all the earnestness that I have, to become His. Then, *of course*, you will dress to please Him. We who are Christians have our own fashions given to us—the robe of humility, the ornament of a meek and quiet spirit—sobriety and modesty in all our outward apparel, because *He* would have us so. We like to please the taste of any one we love—husband, or father, or mother—in what we wear, and we Christians may thus always dress with the thought of pleasing our Master. So about Missionary contributions. I do not press upon you the duty of giving to our Missionary collection. I do not see why those among you who do not know what a precious thing the Gospel of Jesus Christ is for their own souls, should deny themselves to send it to others. I would rather you did not feel obliged to do it, rather that you should not give to please me, or from any other motive. You have not yet a real part in the concern.

"On you, however, who *are* Christ's, who have come to Him, who are living for Him, who are daily drawing from His fulness grace for the day's need, on you who have heard Him say, 'Thy sins are forgiven thee: go in peace,' I do not *need* to press the matter. It is your own affair. You have an opportunity of helping forward your dear Redeemer's kingdom, and you feel you cannot help thus showing your love to Him who so loved you. You have an opening laid before you for sending life to souls sunk in darkness and death, and you cannot help longing that they should hear of the love which has won *you*, which has pardoned *you*, which has saved *you*. *Of course* you are Missionaries in your own homes, for you are Christians. *Of course* you will, so far as you may be able, do something to spread the glory of Jesus, and to send the message of love wherever you can. It lies between you and Him who, for your sakes, became poor, that you through His poverty might become rich. To you the voice comes from the heathen lands—

"'O you who *have* life—you who fear not to die,
Send us help from afar, and give heed to our cry:
That to you in death's hour the thought may be given—
I have brought some to Christ who will meet me in heaven.'"

Dr. Chalmers, in his noble words concerning the newness of life belonging to an acceptance of Christ's offer of salvation, has spoken of *the expulsive power of a new affection* as that which must cause the ways of this world " in the which ye also walked some time past when ye lived in them," to become tasteless and unattractive to the Christian. May we not also speak of the *impulsive* power of that new affection? Certainly, in some Bible-classes, it has proved a reality. The " riches of liberality," which have testified to the constraining power of the love of Jesus in the hearts of their Christian members, have reminded those connected with them of some to whom the Apostle wrote that they were "forward a year ago." The Missionary subscriptions, often sent in with the simple label, "*From one of the Bible-class,*" have been not unfrequently in gold; while home Missionary efforts have afforded a daily opportunity of self-denying testimony to the love of Him who first loved us.

But having, we trust, established the point that those who are, as teachers, trying to stir up Missionary earnestness among their class, will do well to see to the rooting and grounding of all such earnestness in the love of Christ, we would by no means stop there. Starting from the general desire to help forward Missionary work, which must spring from the constraining power of that love, the teacher will try to vivify and give increased interest to these desires, by carefully directing the sympathies of his class towards specific and distinct objects of Missionary effort, and by himself acting as their guide to varied fields of Missionary enterprise.

And we here come to a point on which many of the teacher fraternity will find reason for some self-inquiry. What as to *our own* Missionary knowledge? How far is it connected and thorough? It devolves upon us to render the Missionary interest of our classes intelligent and distinct, as well as deeply-rooted; and is it not our too common experience that, while sensible of the duty of supporting Missionary work in general, our acquaintance with the history, with the chronology, the growth, and the facts of particular missions, is slight and confused. An anecdote from this mission, and an anecdote from that; Bishop Crowther's story from West Africa, and some histories of success from Tinnevelly; reminiscences of the Mutiny; crocodiles, and Suttee in India, and descriptions of heroic strife against ice, snow, and heathenism in America:—these stores, increased from time to time by Missionary addresses at the meetings, or by anecdotes cut out from a newspaper or report, too often represent the stock in trade of our Missionary knowledge, sometimes of so heterogeneous a nature as hardly to allow of classification.

And it is this want of *thoroughness* in the study of Missionary history which tells upon our own warmth of interest in the subject, as well as upon our teaching. English and French and Roman and Grecian history are worthy of careful and diligent research; but the advancement of the Kingdom which is not of this world, the long continuation of the Acts of the Apostles, which is being lived and written over the earth in our time, as it was in those of our fathers—this is a study which we too often push into a corner. The newspaper carries the day over the Missionary records; we do not realise the treasure which will be yielded to patient and intelligent digging for spoil in the wide fields which they represent, and, in our heart of hearts, are inclined to consider the task a dry and dull one.

Which of us could fire our class into enthusiasm by a connected history of the "Great Britain of Africa"— that Madagascar, whereof the records contain instances of heroism as lofty, of faithfulness as undying, as any that has ever glorified the world's history? And yet this history so belongs to our own day as to have had its beginning as late as the year 1819. Which of us could stir up the sympathies of our hearers with a consecutive narration of the living evidence to the power of a living Spirit where the Christian colony of Metlahkahtla borders the blue Pacific; where the native Churches of the Chinese "Happy City" grow and multiply under the sensible influence of that same outpoured Comforter; where among the Arrian tribes

A MISSIONARY SPIRIT IN THE BIBLE-CLASS. 183

the Water of Life has flowed forth from "the place of the Four Plowings"; where the memories of Noble in the Telugu country, and of Thomas in the Tinnevelly district, and of Sargent in Travancore, and of countless others who "climbed the steep ascent of heaven through peril, toil, and pain," are preserved in lasting monuments, in living Churches, in schools and colleges, in advanced outposts of the army of the Kingdom, and have as trophies thousands of souls brought from darkness into Gospel light.

This is not the place for a full entering upon the best method of obtaining Missionary knowledge, nor, in all probability, will any such suggestions be regarded as needful. But we maintain that, to infuse interest on the subject into his class, the teacher must be willing to give many an hour of patient research to thus studying history in her highest aspects; and we are willing confidently to affirm that he who, first taking a skeleton chart* of the history of a particular Mission *from the beginning*, step by step fills it up

* The Chronological Chart of the Church Missionary Society will furnish an excellent basis. As a handbook, containing skeleton histories of all missions, *From Pole to Pole*, by Mr. J. Hassell, of the Home and Colonial School Society, published by Nisbet, is invaluable. It has the additional recommendation of furnishing a list of all books published on particular missions. "*The Church Missionary Juvenile Instructor*" is the cheapest and simplest Church Missionary Magazine for circulation in Bible-classes; the cost being only one halfpenny monthly; and the information suitable for all.

from memoirs, from volumes of Reports, and from every other source within his reach, thus furnishing himself at last with its connected history up to present days, will find the hours slip by as he advances in his task and will discover that the work is well worthy of his best abilities.

To a certain extent, he will be able to carry his class with him into the field which he is engaged in exploring, and will probably discover that by using illustrations, giving anecdotes, and mingling consecutive teaching concerning one particular Mission, from time to time, with his scriptural instruction, he will do far more to animate their interest and to give satisfying Missionary information than by gathering materials from more varied sources.

Let us suppose, for instance, a series of lessons from the Parables of Matt. xiii. How strikingly might every one of them be illustrated by chronologically consecutive narratives and anecdotes from some Missionary history, from the first sowing of the good seed in the field, to the closing parable of the net gathering in the fish good and bad. Slowly, perhaps, but distinctly, there will grow up in the minds of the class an acquaintance with the leading features of that Mission. Books concerning it will be lent to those wishing to know more; and the offer of lending these will often make an excellent pretext for inviting to the teacher's house some whom he may wish to see alone. Often, at such times, the pointing out the place on the map, and the exhibition of some Missionary sketches or photographs, will furnish a pleasant and easy introduction to more personal conversation.

On occasion of the Quarterly or Annual Parochial Missionary Meetings, the teacher will endeavour to stir up an enthusiasm amongst his hearers for the work to be represented amongst them. It is a good plan, when possible, to tell them in advance of the Missions from which the deputation have come, and to enkindle their interest by some anecdotes or personal account of their work. Another incitement is the preparation of the hymns for the Church service and meetings, in which, probably, the musical members will like to take special part. In some cases, especially when the teacher happens to belong to the clergyman's family, it will be possible to enlist the Missionary as a visitor to the Bible-class; and his presence among them, even though but for a short time, and a slight description from his own lips of his life and work, will do much to rivet the interest and earnestness of its members.

The plan of a Missionary working-party is in some places feasible, and affords a royal opportunity for the maintenance of Missionary spirit; but its consideration hardly belongs to these pages.

One plan, found very helpful and uniting in the

support of earnestness in the growth of our Redeemer's kingdom, has been that of agreeing every Christmas to make one Missionary station—generally a solitary and cheerless one—a subject of private and united prayer, the teacher and the class pleading very specially for a Christmas blessing on the Missionary himself, and on his work; and asking for the new year that the "Peace on earth and good-will towards men" may indeed be a message of life to those among whom he labours. News from that station seems, always after, to come as news from a place in which all have a vested interest.

In drawing these chapters to a close, the writer feels that a word ought to be said concerning the *discouragements of Bible-class teaching.*

For it has some peculiarly its own. It seems like the last opportunity time. The trifling of a child's nature may give to the Sunday-school teacher less anxiety than otherwise would be the case, from the hope that the putting away of childish things will come with advancing years. But we feel as if to us in our Bible-class work the very outposts of influence were committed; as if we alone now stood between those for whom it has been given to us so earnestly to care, and the throwing aside of all the sacred associations which with church and school influences we have endeavoured to weave around them. And when one member leaves or becomes careless, and another is led into sin and shame, and a third attends in a trifling and irreverent spirit, and a fourth openly turns his back upon the friend who would win him for Christ, the heart sinks, and we feel as if we had put our hand to work beyond our power, and we are brought to our knees in discouragement and humiliation of spirit.

Brought to our knees. Ah! that is the safest place. Brought to the foot of the Cross; constrained to start afresh, and to toil afresh, and to hope afresh, and to love afresh, from viewing afresh that Love which wearies not. "Therefore turn thou to thy God, and wait on thy God continually." It is His affair; He will renew our strength. He knows all—our failings in our work, our self-will, our weakness, our inconsistencies; knows all, and yet loves better than He knows. And still the message to the Church of Philadelphia is uttered for those who have but a little strength and yet have not denied His name.

And in all our discouragements, let us remember that we have a living Word, a living Spirit, a living Saviour, and an unchangeable promise. The endeavour must be ours, but the results are God's. And though some among us may here see but scant fruit of their labours, let us trust Him for the gathering and the harvest, whose voice shall in a little while sound forth the proclamation, "Call the Labourers!"

WE must leave it for a while,
　　The seed which we have sown ;
The spring-tide will not smile
　　Until wintry months have flown :
The land is not asleep
　　'Neath the mantle of her snows ;
And roots are striking deep
　　While the storm of winter blows :
When April comes to earth,
　　Clouds and sunshine in her sky,
The seedling will spring forth ;
　　We shall see it by-and-by.

We stand upon the shore
　　Whence the stately ships go forth
From the East to bring us store,
　　And full cargoes from the North ;
But years may come and go
　　While the watchers look in vain,
Till the children murmur low,
　　" They will ne'er return again !"
And o'er the pathless sea
　　Their mother strains her eye,
Saying, "We must patient be !
　　They are coming by-and-by !"

The message which we sent
　　To call the wanderer home,—
We wearied till it went ;
　　But the answer has not come.
And early in the day
　　And in the evening late,
Hoping still, we softly say,
　　" We must trust and we must wait !"

And at each glad New Year
　We whisper with a sigh,
"The spring will bring him here;
　We shall see him by-and-bye!"

We must work and we must wait,
　With patient heart and will,
Though the harvest may be late,
　Though the promise tarry still;
Though no vessels we discern,
　Bringing tidings to our shore
Of the wanderers' return
　Through the message which they bore.
Yet, not seeing, we believe
　In a Word which cannot die;
Our times with God we leave;
　We must wait till by-and-by!

THE END.

www.ingramcontent.com/pod-product-compliance
Lightning Source LLC
Chambersburg PA
CBHW020841160426
43192CB00007B/740